A Leap of Faith

A Leap of Faith

How Martin McGuinness and I Worked Together for Peace

DAVID LATIMER

With a foreword by Bernie McGuinness

This book is dedicated to the memory of Martin McGuinness, my dear departed friend, who showed us how to make a way out of no way and transform dark yesterdays into bright tomorrows.

The author is donating his royalties from this book to the North West Cancer Centre, where Martin was treated for Amyloidosis. The North West Cancer Centre provides state-of-the-art therapy to patients with cancer who live on either side of the border. As deputy First Minister of the NI Executive Martin was centrally involved in the commissioning and delivery of this unit, which is a model of cross-community and cross-border cooperation and has resulted in tangible benefits to the people of the north-west of Ireland.

First published in 2018 by Blackstaff Press
an imprint of Colourpoint Creative Ltd, Colourpoint House,
Jubilee Business Park, 21 Jubilee Road,
Newtownards, BT23 4YH

Printed and bound by CPI Group UK Ltd, Croydon CRO 4YY

A CIP catalogue for this book is available from the British Library

ISBN 978-1-78073-180-3
www.blackstaffpress.com

Contents

With Bernie McGuinness.

Foreword
Bernie McGuinness

David tells the story of an occasion when, after one of their many meetings, he turned to Martin and said, 'Martin, I really value our friendship.'

Looking him straight in the eye, Martin responded by saying, 'David, I treasure our friendship.'

Martin did treasure his friendship with David. It was important to him. And it was a truly remarkable friendship. On paper it shouldn't have worked. Friendship between a Presbyterian church leader and a prominent republican would have seemed, to many, impossible, or at least highly unlikely, in a society emerging from conflict.

But it did work and, over a period of ten years, Martin and David managed to forge a deep and abiding friendship, one that surprised many and shocked some.

Indeed, their friendship came at a cost. It wasn't well received by some. David lost members of his congregation angered at his willingness to reach out to a republican.

However, they continued to keep moving forward, taking risks, challenging mind-sets, pushing boundaries and breaking moulds, confident in their conviction that the politics of reconciliation was key to what they both wanted

– a shared future devoid of the recrimination and division of the past.

They ploughed a unique and sometimes lonely furrow. It wasn't always easy. But they were always determined to ensure the flame of partnership, reconciliation and working together remained burning bright.

It is fitting that David should write this book as it gives a special insight into what was a groundbreaking relationship.

David and Martin understood that agreement and compromise require partnership and, crucially, a willingness to take risks. They are an inspiring example of peace and reconciliation for others to follow.

During my childhood in Dromore.

1
Early Impressions

I can vividly recall being with a few mates in my home town of Dromore in County Down on a Saturday evening in August 1969. One of them had been listening to the radio before leaving home and he informed us that riots had broken out on the streets of Londonderry following the Apprentice Boys' annual parade.

In the 1950s, when I was a young boy, the world seemed a big place. Even other places in Northern Ireland, such as Enniskillen, Portrush and Londonderry, sounded far away. Like so many people back then, I hadn't ever ventured far from home. Dromore was a quiet, mainly Protestant town where nothing much out of the ordinary ever happened. In addition to the usual mix of Protestant churches, there was 'the chapel,' as we called it, and a separate primary school for Catholics.

After primary school in Dromore, I attended Banbridge Technical College where, for the first time, I sat alongside students with first names such as Patsy and Seamus – names that were quite different to those I was accustomed to. We got along well together. Religious differences only arose when we were divided into our various denominational groups for instruction with priests and ministers who came into the college. Even this didn't prove to be an obstacle – it was just a period in the college timetable when we weren't all in the same classroom.

Around the age of fifteen I became aware of Ian Paisley. He came to Dromore and surrounding towns to preach at special 'drumhead' services and to conduct old-time gospel campaigns. Huge crowds flocked to hear him speak. One of my group of friends always bought a copy of the *Protestant Telegraph*, Paisley's newspaper, which we read and discussed during the bus journey to college in Banbridge. On numerous occasions, I attended rallies in Ballynahinch, Dromara, Dromore and Hillsborough, at which Paisley verbally attacked the Rome-ward trend of Irish Presbyterianism and denounced the Pope as the Antichrist. Listening to Paisley's words helped shape my thinking and certainly coloured my view of Roman Catholics who, we were led to believe, all supported the IRA and wanted a united Ireland.

It was on 7 April 1976 that the Troubles arrived in the sleepy, off-the-beaten-track town of Dromore and nobody could understand why. The Herrons were a good Presbyterian family who owned a drapery shop that served all the community. Periodically my mother took me there to buy my shirts, school blazer, overcoat and trousers. On that day in 1976, someone had slipped an incendiary device into the shop. It later exploded, and William and Elizabeth Herron, and their twenty-seven-year-old daughter Noeline, lost their lives in the ensuing blaze.

The Herrons were buried in the graveyard that adjoined the Presbyterian church I attended. Two of their sons, Alastair and Derrick, were well known to me. We were all members of the 3rd Dromore Boys' Brigade Company. The people of Dromore were well and truly shaken – not just by the deaths of the Herrons, but by the sickening manner in which their lives were abruptly ended.

When I left school after completing my O levels, I started work as a clerk at the Electricity Board for Northern Ireland (EBNI) headquarters on Belfast's Malone Road. Encouraged to continue and develop my education, I availed of the company's day-release scheme, which enabled me to attend college one day a week. In this way, I obtained both Ordinary National and Higher National Certificates in Business Studies. I subsequently enrolled at Queen's University to read Economics, which was offered to part-time students over a five-year period.

While I continued to combine part-time study with full-time work, the company's personnel department invited applications for the position of trainee systems analyst in a newly formed organisation and methods department. I was appointed to one of these positions.

It was while I was working in Belfast, on 17 February 1978 to be exact, that one of the worst atrocities of the Troubles took place. More than four hundred people were attending an annual dinner dance at the La Mon House hotel on the outskirts of Belfast. An IRA blast incendiary ignited, engulfing the hotel in flames and claiming the lives of twelve Protestant civilians, including three sets of young married couples, and injuring more than thirty.

Arriving at work the following Monday, I learned that two of the people who lost their lives in the La Mon inferno were Ian and Liz McCracken, both of whom worked at EBNI headquarters office. I knew both Ian and Liz well: every day I would be in conversation with one or other of them. Like a great many of their colleagues, I attended their joint funeral service in First Bangor Presbyterian Church. Once again I was confronted by the ugliness of an ideology that included the use of violence.

In 1981, RUC reservist Ronald Pollock – a Dromore man living in Banbridge – was left disabled by an IRA bomb that had been attached to his car. The Pollocks were loyal members of the church I attended. We all knew each other.

The painful deaths and horrifying disfigurements of people I knew were impossible to rationalise. At the time I recall politicians and clergy alike struggling to adequately describe those who committed such depraved acts.

It was during the 1970s that I found myself working in Londonderry Corporation's Electricity Department. My remit was to streamline procedures following the amalgamation of Belfast's and Derry's electricity departments with EBNI to form one single company called the Northern Ireland Electricity Service (NIES). The journey to the city was long and the road was punctuated by bends and bumps. The colleague I was with and I were both more than a little apprehensive about travelling so far north. News coverage suggested the city was in turmoil. To keep safe, we stayed at a hotel ten miles east of the city. As it turned out, we were warmly welcomed and exceptionally well treated throughout our time at the electricity offices, located on the city's busy Strand Road. I have nothing but positive memories of those early visits.

The office was directly opposite the police station. Bomb scares were a frequent occurrence. It was not unusual to arrive late to work because of police and army checkpoints, or the Craigavon Bridge being closed. Neither was it unusual to be evacuated from the office while police and army combed the area looking for explosive devices.

In spite of this I was enjoying my job: the working conditions were excellent. In addition to being in Derry, I also spent time working in the NIES area offices in Coleraine and Omagh. I was looking forward to a career with the NIES and the guarantee of a generous pension on retirement.

But even though I was content in my work, there was something going on in my mind that was difficult to dismiss. I wasn't seeing bright lights flashing or hearing voices, but deep inside there was something pulling me in the direction of the ordained ministry. Eventually I plucked up the courage to resign from my job and, in 1979, I left the security of the NIES to begin studying as a mature student at Union Theological College in Belfast. Three years later I took an assistantship in Railway Street Presbyterian Church in Lisburn. After a year I moved to become minister of the rural congregations of Glascar and Donaghmore in County Down where I remained until 1988, when I became the minister of First Derry Presbyterian Church and of the County Donegal congregation of Monreagh.

© Derry Journal

First Derry at the time when extensive security measures were in place. The doors on either side of the central door are sealed with cement for security reasons.

2
Life in Derry

First Derry is on Upper Magazine Street, in the heart of Derry city centre, separated from the nationalist Bogside by the city's historic walls. When I arrived, the church was tightly wrapped in a security blanket. High rusted wire fencing surrounded the perimeter of the building. There were bulletproof windowpanes and steel shutters on every door. The place looked like a picture from a war zone. Sadly, all the security hid the beautiful building, which was an important piece of the city's built heritage, dating back to 1780, distinguished by four fluted columns with Corinthian capitals. Derry itself had taken quite a pounding since the riots of 1969 spilled over into street violence. Scarred spaces were everywhere and clear for everybody to see.

I remember being handed a big bunch of keys – I needed all of them to get into the church building – and thinking to myself that it would be easier getting into Fort Knox. Maybe I should have been put off by the location of the church, its appearance and the need for such extensive security, but none of this made me waver from my decision to come to Derry. Some clergy found it hard to see why a young man would come to an old man's church, as they put it.

First Derry had been weakened by the Troubles. As a result, the Presbytery of Derry formed a new link with

Monreagh, a small Presbyterian church located just over the border in east Donegal. I was the first minister to serve with this new arrangement in place, which – it was hoped – would bolster a formerly strong city-centre church.

Very soon after being installed I started to hear the heartbreaking details of a congregation virtually brought to its knees by the Troubles. Five parishioners, all deemed legitimate targets because they were serving with the RUC and UDR, had been murdered by the IRA. The building itself – which had been a sacred space for Presbyterians since the first church opened in 1690 – was despised by republicans in the 1970s and 80s. It was regularly bombarded with bottles, bricks and stones – all launched from the other side of the historic city walls.

The River Foyle divides the city. The west bank, referred to as the Cityside and home to First Derry, has always been more nationalist in composition. The east bank of the river, which has always been more unionist, is known as the Waterside. Protestants living, working and worshipping on the Cityside started moving to the Waterside, believing it to be a safer place to live. By the time I arrived in 1988, First Derry had become a numerically weaker congregation due to the exodus of Protestants from the Cityside, in large part because of the IRA.

It was at this time that I was learning more about the Troubles in Derry and hearing more about people like Martin McGuinness. Nobody at First Derry had a good word to say about him, and some bereaved families believed that he was responsible for the deaths of their loved ones.

In my role as a Territorial Army chaplain, a position that I held until 2010, I was occasionally invited to Ebrington Barracks, the headquarters of the British army in the city. Casual interaction with officers introduced me to their perspective on Martin McGuinness and his republican colleagues.

Sometime after moving to Derry, I was driving up Carlisle Road towards the Diamond and saw Martin McGuinness for the first time in the flesh, walking along the footpath. He was wearing what seemed like a tweed jacket. 'Why don't the police lift that man?' I said to myself. 'How can he freely walk about?'

Soon after my installation, I called at the church to meet the bowling club, who held the only remaining weeknight church activity. Every other evening activity had stopped. The Sunday evening services were halted on the advice of the army – who told us that we were making ourselves a target by having the lights on at night. Cars parked at the church were being damaged. The fear of being caught up in a street riot deterred attendances at every other activity.

When I went to see the bowling club, I had just been to a nearby car wash and my yellow Ford Escort was gleaming. Parking my car outside the church gates on Upper Magazine Street, I popped into the church hall. About an hour later, a lady entered the hall and enquired who owned the yellow car. I told her that it was mine and she informed me it had been hit with stones. When I went outside I was speechless. The roof, bonnet and some of the doors had all been cratered by large pieces of masonry that had been thrown over the walls. The car was a mess. This was a different kind of welcome – one I could have done without.

In addition to the bricks, stones and bottles raining down on the church, and the occasional burned-out car on the street, the building was also attacked with paint bombs that splashed the facade and fluted pillars with different colours. One Sunday morning, a parishioner leaving the church, which was disfigured with splashes of paint, said to me, 'David, if you don't remove the blue and white, we might end up with the colours of the Union flag!'

Pastoring the linked congregation of Monreagh and First Derry kept me busy. In the early years I focused on both my churches as I sought to get to know the people, listen to their stories and be a friend. The members of the congregations, especially in the city, were notably scattered – the result of parishioners moving to places such as Bready, Claudy, Drumahoe and Eglinton. Only a handful of families remained on the Cityside.

When First Derry was severely damaged by a petrol bomb in 1983, the parishioners of Long Tower Church, the closest Catholic church to First Derry, organised a collection, which amounted to £1,100 and was quietly handed over as a gesture of support. Soon after my arrival, Long Tower's Father Michael Collins invited me to share a broadcast of readings and prayers on BBC Radio Foyle for Good Friday. This became an annual event and allowed a friendship with my neighbouring Catholic colleagues to evolve. Being invited to address the Long Tower's Christmas service during the mid-1990s was a new and special experience and paved the way for the friendship to grow. St Patrick's Day lunches at the parish parochial house on Abercorn Road were sumptuous and memorable affairs. My wife Margaret and I returned the favour by having the priests for lunch at the manse on August bank holidays. These informal and relaxed events allowed all of us to talk about our two communities, the conflict, our faith and the many things that united us.

★

The 1998 Good Friday Agreement encouraged us to begin dismantling some of the security paraphernalia around the church. By the start of the third millennium, the wire fencing had all been removed and the heavy metal doors were gone. For the first time since I had taken over as minister of Derry's oldest Presbyterian congregation, the building actually looked like a church.

There was a noticeably buoyant mood among the congregation. Larger attendances at Sunday worship led to the reopening of the church gallery, which had been shut since 1969. The congregation was on the crest of a wave until, in 2002, a structural survey uncovered a severe outbreak of dry rot. To my dismay, it soon transpired that the church was unsafe and we were forced to close it.

A church that had survived wars, economic downturns and the trauma of the Troubles was now out of action because of dry rot. Amazingly the congregation was undaunted by the prospect of closure. Being chair of Fountain Primary School board of governors enabled me to quickly secure a temporary place for worship. The first few Sundays saw the assembly hall full to capacity. There was a palpable sense of camaraderie amongst the First Derry membership. Everyone made a big effort to attend worship. While none of us knew what the future held, there was certainly no talk of First Derry closing.

Carlisle Road Methodist Church on the Cityside, aware of our plight, generously offered us their building, and for nine years, the Presbyterian family gathered there every Sunday for worship.

During the late autumn of 2007, I was visiting families in the Waterside and while I was at one home, one of my congregation told me that First Derry had been hit with paint again. On my way home, I drove across to Upper

Magazine Street to see the damage for myself and, sure enough, fresh paint had been splashed onto the front of the building.

As a church, our normal reaction was to keep our heads down and say nothing. I returned home around 11 p.m., deflated by this latest paint attack, thinking to myself that some things just don't change and that we'd simply have to grin and bear it.

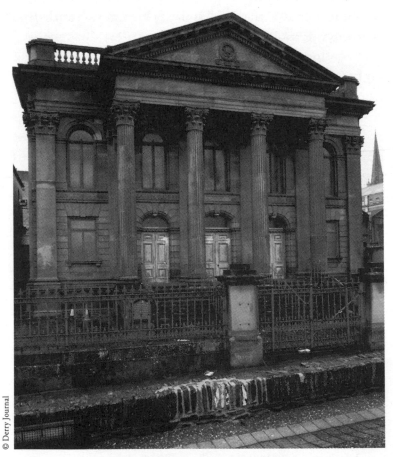

© Derry Journal

First Derry after the paint-bomb attack.

Next morning, I woke early. The paint-spattered church was on my mind. Happily, Derry was becoming more popular with tourists, and the historic city walls were a key attraction. Every day many visitors were passing the church. Concluding that my defaced church was not sending out the right kind of message to the world, I decided it was time to go public.

I arrived at BBC Radio Foyle and asked if I could take part in their early morning news programme. The paint bombing became the lead story. The interviewer's first question was straight to the point: 'Reverend, your church has been hit again with paint. What are you for doing?'

I replied: 'I want to appeal to the only person in this city who can do anything about it.'

'And who might that be, Reverend?'

'It's a man who in the past wore a hat that gave him a lot of authority and I don't think he's lost any of that authority. The man is Martin McGuinness.'

I wondered if I had done the right thing, and what would happen.

A short while after the radio interview, to my great surprise, I received a telephone call from Sinn Féin letting me know that Martin McGuinness would like to meet me and asking if I'd be willing to see him that same morning to discuss the situation at my church. I agreed. First to arrive was local Sinn Féin MLA Raymond McCartney. Then, at 10.30 a.m., a ministerial car, with Martin McGuinness sitting in the front seat, stopped outside the front gates of the church.

As soon as he got out of the car, he approached me with an outstretched hand, and we firmly shook hands for the first time. We walked up the front steps to inspect the paint damage. Outside the closed front doors, we once again shook hands and photographers, who were by now at the church, notified by Sinn Féin with my agreement, captured me warmly welcoming the former IRA leader to First Derry.

I was feeling slightly nervous about meeting Martin McGuinness and I thought it might help if we talked over a cup of tea. So, between the interview and going to the church, I had packed some scones my wife had baked, along with a flask of hot water, cups and milk. Arriving at the church, about five or ten minutes before the meeting was due to begin, I noticed I'd forgotten butter. I dashed across to the nearby Tower Hotel where a receptionist kindly gave me a handful of little individual butter packs. Sorted.

With Martin McGuinness and Raymond McCartney
outside the church.

Leaving the front steps of the church, Martin and I made our way around by the rear of the church building to the kitchen where everything was in place. I vividly remember concentrating on pouring hot water into the cups for my guests, stirring in the tea bags and struggling with the scones. The packs of butter had been taken straight from the freezer and were like concrete, resulting in the freshly baked scones slowly disintegrating. What a disaster.

Totally unaware that my clumsy kitchen skills were being observed, I heard a voice behind me. 'David, if you do the scones, I'll look after the tea.' Turning round, I saw Martin approach the worktop and finish making the tea. I was momentarily taken aback. To be honest, I'm not sure what I expected but I certainly got a surprise when he helped with the refreshments. I've often reflected on that moment in the kitchen that I now consider seminal. Somehow it allowed me to recognise the common humanity we shared.

As we started to eat the scones and sip our tea, I said to Martin: 'How long have you got?'

'I have as long as you need,' he replied.

Our conversation, which extended to about an hour, turned to the concerns and insecurities of my congregation, and it quickly became clear that I was in the company of a person who wanted his Presbyterian neighbours to have a peaceful environment to meet and worship.

Martin's primary focus was the paint-bomb attacks and how they were impacting on church activities and parishioners' morale. However, before leaving, he asked about the condition of the church and the reasons for the property not being fit for purpose.

I explained that a section of the church had been

engulfed in flames as a direct result of a petrol bomb attack in 1983. Timber specialists inspecting the property in 2002 believed that the dry rot, discovered in the heavy timber roof trusses, was the direct result of the water flooded on to the property by the emergency services to extinguish the fire started by the petrol bomb.

We also talked about the church members' increasing anxiety about how we were going to pay for the restoration, which was becoming frighteningly expensive. Steel towers had been erected inside the church to prevent the roof from collapsing. While the church had absorbed this cost, there was no way that the congregation, by itself, could embark on a restoration project that was predicted to cost well in excess of £1 million.

Martin seemed just as interested in helping us to reopen First Derry as he was in stopping the paint-bomb attacks.

'I can see your church from my upstairs window,' he told me during our conversation. Feeling as though he was keeping an eye on us from his home reassured me and made me feel as though his commitment to help us was genuine.

Before leaving, Martin said he'd like to keep in touch and gave me a mobile number that he said I could use any time. Raymond remarked that I was privileged – that Martin didn't give that number to many people.

The success of the meeting came as a complete surprise to me. This kind of meeting wasn't even meant to happen because the members of the two traditions within the city lived apart from each other. The Troubles had succeeded in opening wounds sufficient to justify one side staying well clear of the other. Yet, Martin McGuinness, despite his past, made that journey from his home in the Bogside to First Derry Church in Upper Magazine Street – a distance of only a few hundred yards as the crow flies, but symbolically equivalent to bringing two continents together. Something quite unthinkable had happened.

A positive result of my first meeting with Martin was an immediate end to the paint-bomb attacks. The fact that they had stopped made it easier for me to explain to the congregation the newspaper photographs of us standing together at the top of First Derry's steps.

A couple of months later I received a surprise phone call from Martin, who wanted to talk further about the problems with the church building. This time we agreed to meet at my home. Even though Martin had given me his personal number, a follow-up meeting had never crossed my mind. We were still strangers. I was nervous about doing this. Notwithstanding, I readily agreed to the meeting. This was his first visit to our home. My wife Margaret was apprehensive and worried, perhaps even a little fearful.

When Martin arrived we shook hands in the hall. I took Martin into the kitchen to meet Margaret, and there was a nervous shaking of hands, but he broke the ice by talking about where we'd all come from, and how long we'd been in Derry, and about our family.

Martin and I went into the sitting room for tea and scones, and a rather formal conversation about eradicating the dry rot and making the church fit for purpose again. It was clear Martin had been doing some research on our behalf, which struck a chord with me because up to that point we had had plenty of promises of help without anything materialising. Martin, however, clearly had practical plans and, as I was to discover, he would go on to do what he said he was going to.

Margaret vividly remembers Martin opening the kitchen door to thank her for the tea and scones and to shake her hand before he left. That gesture made a lovely impression on her. And it wasn't a one-off occurrence – Martin never left our house without speaking with Margaret and expressing appreciation for her hospitality. Afterwards, reflecting on the visit and not quite believing Martin McGuinness had been sitting drinking tea in our home, we both commented on how friendly and pleasant he was. Visiting a Protestant home close to Newbuildings, a relatively loyalist village, can't have been straightforward for him. We were relieved the meeting had gone as well as it had.

Once we'd had these couple of meetings, Martin's and my paths crossed more often. We'd frequently bump into each other at various civic and public events around the city. Martin always made a point of getting across the room to speak with me. He didn't need to do this, especially given that so many people were always clamouring to shake his hand and get a word with him. We were progressively becoming more relaxed in each other's company. Moreover, updates he gave me during these brief encounters regarding possible funding sources for First Derry convinced me that he had not forgotten about my worries about the church.

This was a side to Martin that I picked up on more and more as we got to know each other better – he never took any notes, but he never forgot to act on any of his promises.

In my army uniform before leaving for Afghanistan.

3

Army Chaplaincy in Afghanistan

On Ash Wednesday in 2008, I received a telephone call at teatime to inform me that I would be accompanying 204 (NI) Field Hospital RAMC (V) to Afghanistan in June as chaplain. I had been with the unit since 1984, but this was a big surprise because I had been led to believe that a regular army chaplain would take this role during the unit's deployment. In fact, the commanding officer particularly wanted me to accompany the unit – they needed somebody they knew and could trust.

Territorial Army medical units from around the UK were being deployed to run the medical facility at Camp Bastion in Helmand Province. When it became known that our unit would be included in the revolving rota to run this medical facility, intensive training to prepare all of us for our varied roles went into full swing.

Martin promised to pray for me and for my safe return while I was in Afghanistan, something he said not just privately to me, but to the press. He also told me, 'We will keep the good ship First Derry moving forward until you get back.' No other church, civic or political figure said anything like this. It concerned me that I was leaving First Derry at the worst possible time but my fears were allayed by the knowledge that Northern Ireland's deputy First Minister would, in my absence, be keeping the church's restoration high on his busy agenda. It was what I needed to hear before leaving the city – First Derry was in safe hands.

Much to my surprise, my mobilisation as a British army chaplain to Afghanistan generated considerable interest in Derry. Close to the time of my departure, local papers interviewed me at length. BBC Radio Foyle devoted a major part of a morning news and current affairs programme to my mobilisation. A wide-ranging, gentle discussion explored how chaplaincy in a theatre of war might differ from an NHS chaplain's role. A photograph of myself wearing a British army desert uniform, including combat helmet, was subsequently posted on the BBC's website and I was also interviewed at length for a local newspaper, the *Derry Journal*.

A few days after arriving in Helmand province, I was told that a senior chaplain would be flying in from Kandahar for a meeting with me. Presuming this to be a courtesy visit by the boss to bid me welcome, I happily made my way at the appointed time to the church – which, like virtually everything else inside the perimeter walls of the Afghan desert military base, was a brown canvas tent. This particular chaplain was known to me. We'd met on numerous occasions at conferences in the Royal Army Chaplaincy Department Centre outside London. We'd gelled, I thought, reasonably well. An ordained Anglican clergyman, he now held the rank of lieutenant colonel.

From the outset it was clear this was not a courtesy call to welcome me to Camp Bastion. Quite the opposite. News of my BBC Radio Foyle conversation and *Derry Journal* interview had reached military headquarters in Kandahar. The senior chaplain had dropped into Camp Bastion to reprimand me for 'carelessly divulging', as he put it, 'information to the media prior to leaving home that could compromise the security of mobilised personnel.'

I knew that I hadn't divulged anything that wasn't already in the public domain; and at that point, I had certainly never been told that I shouldn't be talking to the media. I attempted to explain that, in a city like Derry, with its vivid memories of British army aggression, the local media showing interest in and support for a local Protestant minister donning the uniform of the British army, was actually something to be welcomed. The senior chaplain had no interest whatever in Derry or how nationalists and republicans perceived a minister from their city dressed in army fatigues and serving with the armed forces of the British Crown. The conversation, which lasted for about forty minutes, ended just as frostily as it had started. Later that night, struggling to fall sleep, I felt like I was being spied upon and I wondered if there was uneasiness among the higher echelons because of my acquaintance with Martin.

A number of UK TV channels visited Camp Bastion during our tour of duty. My intention was to keep my friendship with Martin fairly quiet while I was in Afghanistan. As it turned out, however, that was easier said than done. On two occasions I recall a senior officer saying to TV journalists as I walked through the hospital complex that they should talk to me because I was friendly with Martin. My response was to smile and keep walking rather than stop and risk drawing unnecessary attention – I didn't want an evolving friendship to be upset for reasons of cheap and unhelpful publicity.

Throughout my tour of duty, mobile phones were banned so regular contact with family and friends was curtailed. Halfway into the tour, I heard from home that Martin's mother, Peggy, had died. I immediately forwarded my condolences, including a short prayer, to Martin on a British army 'bluey' that I addressed to him at Stormont.

In my four months as a hospital chaplain, I stood alongside 56 body bags and witnessed 1,098 people passing through the hospital facility. Many of those I came into contact with had injuries that ranged from life-changing to life-ending. While deployment training in the weeks leading up to our departure had been thorough, nothing could have prepared me for the sights, smells and sounds of war.

On my first day in the hospital, I was called to the mortuary tent – referred to in army parlance as 'Rose Cottage'. An American soldier had been fatally wounded by an improvised explosive device (IED). One of my 204 colleagues drew the zip back on the body bag; my eyes were tightly closed. I then heard a voice saying, 'This one's not too bad, Davy. This guy has only lost a leg!' I opened one eye to glance towards the body bag, then opened the other eye to see a young soldier lying like he was sleeping with a severed leg resting on his chest. It was a horrible sight. I couldn't speak and didn't for quite a while. The commanding officer, recognising the effect the dead soldier was having, took those of us who'd been in the mortuary tent to the nearby juice bar where we sat in stunned silence. This was bad but very soon it was to get worse. Much worse.

A week or so later, I was waiting at the hospital entrance as the latest cargo of broken bodies were being flown in from the desert. One of the ambulances deviated from the normal dusty track towards the mortuary tent. On board was a British soldier who had been killed by a dreaded IED. As the stretcher bearers were transferring the body from the ambulance into Rose Cottage, one of them remarked: 'This one's a bit light – it's not going to be easy.' Once the zip was drawn back, the full horror of the young soldier's injuries could be seen. He had blonde hair; his face, hair and jacket were all smeared with sandy desert dust; he looked as if he was sleeping; there were no visible signs of fear or pain. But, horror of horrors, only half of this young soldier, who resembled a schoolboy in uniform, was in the body bag. Everything else, from just below his chest, had been blown away. Silence filled Rose Cottage. Soldiers, hardened by their service in places such as Bosnia and Kosovo, were in shock, as I was.

A voice interrupted the silence.'Padre, will you say something?

Help, I thought. What on earth can I say?

Standing around the opened body bag inside the small mortuary tent were a couple of military police officers, an army doctor, a photographer, a colleague of the deceased and the stretcher bearers. I was firmly standing on virgin soil. Nothing in my life had prepared me for this moment. I felt very inadequate as a Christian minister. Saying anything religious in this setting seemed bizarre and pointless. Finding my voice, eventually, I said, 'None of us should be witnessing this sight. It's evil.' I don't quite know how I was able to compose myself sufficiently to continue. 'Beyond the walls of Bastion, there are people devoted to death and destruction; here, inside Bastion, there are people completely committed to saving life. I believe goodness is stronger than evil and life is stronger than death.' My speech ended with a fumbling prayer commending the soul of the deceased soldier to the safe keeping of an eternal God. As soon as I said 'Amen', the formalities associated with death on the battlefield resumed. This was harrowing work. Trying to sleep, even after an eighteen-hour day, wasn't easy.

Late one afternoon, the body of a badly wounded Danish soldier arrived at the hospital complex. With lightning speed, this big guy was transferred from the field ambulance on to a trolley and taken along the corridor towards intensive care. Given the extent of his injuries he was soon on his way to be scanned, and it was during this procedure that he arrested and died. I can vividly recall the body of this Goliath-like man lying motionless on the trolley, with his large feet protruding well over the edge. His desert combat shirt had been torn from his body by the IED explosion to reveal an extensive tattoo of his dog tag, bearing his name, his number and his religion. The links of the chain were also tattooed around his neck. It was a very different but impressive piece of body art.

Three of the soldier's colleagues had accompanied the medical team and me from the moment he arrived at the hospital. Everyone stood still, shocked by his sudden death. The expectation, as always, was that the padre would say something that might calm troubled spirits and offer peace in the midst of a storm. Once again I struggled to speak.

The next morning the soldier's three mates came searching for me. 'Padre,' they exclaimed, 'we want the prayer you used yesterday.'

I asked which one they meant, and they responded without hesitation, 'The Lord, Padre, the Lord.'

That was enough to jog my memory. During the impromptu service, I'd used the words of the Aaronic Blessing. 'Why do you want the words?' I asked.

'That prayer helped us yesterday and we want to send it back with the body as it will help his mummy.'

Immediately I wrote down the prayer for them:

The Lord bless you and keep you.
The Lord make his face to shine upon you, and
    be gracious to you.
The Lord lift up his countenance upon you, and
    give you peace.

A prayer that previously had fallen from my lips on countless occasions suddenly became special to me. In fact, I intentionally wove those simple yet sublime words into the prayer I said with Martin when I came home – which turned out to be the first of many.

Towards the end of our tour of duty, it was reported that we had been part of one of the busiest British military operations since the end of the Second World War. I was weary of seeing broken and dismembered bodies and hugely disturbed by the trauma that ordinary Afghans were experiencing. They were what is euphemistically known as collateral damage. Men, women and children, living in extreme poverty, looked perplexed and puzzled. It was heartbreaking to watch them. This was wrong.

Being in a war zone was shaping my views vis-à-vis the use of force to settle differences. William T. Sherman, who was a United States army general during the American Civil War, once remarked: 'War is cruelty, and you cannot refine it.' Strange how some things just don't change with the passage of time. My experience 150 years later in Afghanistan brought me face to face with the cruelty of war and left me, just as it had left Sherman, 'sick and tired'. War was in no way the solution to anything.

Throughout my time in Camp Bastion, I was writing articles about the job I was doing and forwarding these to journalists in Belfast and Derry who were printing them in their newspapers. This kept people back home informed. By now, I knew to exercise caution but I did not ask for any of my pieces to be officially checked because I felt they did not contain any sensitive details.

One night, after returning from Rose Cottage, where yet another young British soldier's mutilated body had arrived, I sat down with my laptop and began to write. In this article I included the statement, 'At this moment in time, I could not support political decisions that mobilise young men and women to a theatre of war.'

A few days later, about two thirds of the way through our tour, I was informed by the CO that there was disquiet back home about an article I'd sent to a newspaper. I couldn't think what I could have said – it was only when I got home from Afghanistan that I discovered that the unhappiness was generated by one of my newspaper articles. The *Belfast Telegraph* had added the headline, 'Army Padre Says He Can No Longer Support War,' to my article. I didn't believe that this headline was representative of what I had written – although I was deeply concerned about the political decisions that were sending the troops to Afghanistan, my support for my colleagues in Camp Bastion remained profound and resolute. But the damage was done. I would not be overstating it when I say anger was in the air at the NI Chaplains' Office at Army HQ Lisburn and also in England.

During one of several 'interviews without coffee', I was informed that an official in London, having read the *Belfast Telegraph* article, had been jumping up and down saying, 'We must silence this man.' Another had said, 'We must sack him,' only to be told, 'Sir, we can't sack this man. He's friendly with Martin McGuinness.'

I shared this story with Martin at a meeting at my house soon after I returned home. He smiled and said: 'David, that's what happens when we put our heads above the parapet! But it's too late to do anything about it now. The damage is done, they know we're friends.' And he was right. Word was abroad that Martin and I were meeting up and talking, and that was frowned upon by more than a few.

Across the UK it became the custom to organise a thanksgiving service to welcome troops home from their operational tour. Our service was at St Anne's Cathedral in Belfast. Knowing I would be preaching at this service, I began assembling ideas – grabbing a few minutes here and a few minutes there as our time in Afghanistan came to an end. Earlier in the tour a metalsmith had made me a cross using eight empty fifty-calibre bullet shells – this universal symbol of love shaped from grotesque, deadly bits of metal would become the centrepiece for my sermon at St Anne's.

© Diane Magill

On my return from Afghanistan.

On the morning of the service, which was to be followed by the distribution of our campaign medals by Northern Ireland's GOC, everyone gathered at the TA centre to change into desert combats and await transport. A few minutes before we departed, the unit's second-in-command enquired if the CO had spoken to me. When I said no, he left the room. The CO soon arrived and asked me, 'Are you aware you will not be preaching at this morning's service?' I told him I wasn't and he continued, 'Somebody was to tell you. The dean will be preaching. It's got nothing to do with what you've been writing or with the people you're friendly with.' I remember responding with the words, 'Sir, it's got everything to do with my writing and with my friendships but I won't shoot the messenger.'

I was shaken. As the bus made its way along the Malone Road, I stared blankly out through the window seeing nothing. I couldn't believe I was being treated so shabbily.

At the cathedral, I was dressed in desert combats and a preaching scarf. These were the clothes I'd worn when conducting worship and ministering to the wounded and the dead in Camp Bastion. It was also the dress that chaplains wore at sombre repatriation services for mortally wounded servicemen and women. Because I was not wearing robes, I was forbidden by the dean to process with other clergy at the start of the service. Instead, I was taken to my seat. I felt humiliated, to say the least. My part in the service was simply to say a short prayer that had been written by someone else.

The homecoming sermon was delivered by the dean of the cathedral. In the course of his remarks, he made reference to the wonderful work I'd been doing as hospital chaplain in Camp Bastion and how much it had been appreciated. Hearing this didn't make me feel any better. If I'd done such a good job in Camp Bastion why was I barred from speaking in Belfast to the people I'd served with? At the close of the service the dean approached me and said: 'Davy, I couldn't do anything else.' I didn't want to talk about it then. Church politics and personal clerical opinions appeared to rule supreme. It took me quite some time to absorb the heartlessness of the way I was treated both by a leading member of a major Protestant denomination and by the British army. To this very day, it continues to be uncomfortable to contemplate.

My homecoming sermon, which I wrote entirely in the Afghan desert and which I was banned from preaching, is included in the appendices.

Notwithstanding my minimal role in the service, I look back with a great sense of pride at the opportunity of being with doctors, nurses and surgeons, who were working around the clock saving lives and bringing hope to the soldiers engaged in exceptionally difficult work outside the walls of Camp Bastion. To be able to offer words of comfort in a sea of hurt was an extraordinary privilege, and to have been in the company of my colleagues at the darkest times was a huge honour and something that I shall forever be grateful for.

Shortly after the homecoming service, I telephoned Martin to invite him for a catch-up chat at my home. We met on a Saturday morning, which tended to be the best day for both of us. In the past we shook hands whenever we came together. On this occasion, however, as soon as Martin stepped into the hall, he gave me a hug and expressed his delight at having me back in Derry.

Showing Edwin Poots, Minister of the Environment, and Arlene Foster, Minister for Enterprise, Trade and Investment, around First Derry in February 2010.

4

The Presbyterian Church in the Bogside

Within a few days of resuming my pastoral duties, following a period of post-operational tour leave, I received a telephone call inviting me to meet with Andy Best from the Northern Ireland Tourist Board (NITB). During this meeting, which took place in a Ballymena cafe, I was given a letter advising me First Derry had been awarded £1.6 million. What a Christmas present! Presbyterians within Derry's walls were being highly favoured. I shared this good news with the congregation at our weekly service in Carlisle Road Methodist Church in the company of the Moderator of the General Assembly who was our special New Year's guest. Given the proximity of First Derry to Free Derry Corner and the Bogside, I raised a few eyebrows and generated more than a few smiles when I referred to my church on the walls as 'The Presbyterian church in the Bogside'.

The NITB letter was nothing short of great news because, up until my first meeting with Martin, it had looked as if we were on our own and would have to fund a costly repair bill entirely by ourselves. Fortunately for First Derry, this was no longer the case – we were one of six buildings within the Walled City eligible for financial assistance under the Built Heritage Programme. Timely intervention by a largely nationalist/republican city council, on behalf of a Protestant minority group, had successfully paved the way for the allocation of a generous financial package, sanctioned by the NI Executive and administered by NITB.

In addition to talking about First Derry and the various attempts to circumvent obstacles affecting the restoration project, Martin and I started discussing other initiatives that might help to bring our divided city together.

During these informal chats, I discovered just how devoted Martin was to his family. On many occasions he expressed his wish for a future different to the past – one that could be enjoyed by his grandchildren and by all children growing up on either side of the River Foyle. I remember Martin visiting my home while Joanne, my eldest daughter, was there with her one-year-old daughter Gracie. After I'd introduced Martin to Joanne, her first time meeting him, Martin looked at Gracie and said: 'Will you come to me?' He reached out for her and she jumped into his arms. Martin continued to hold Gracie as he talked with Joanne.

Martin with our granddaughter Gracie.

Later, during our conversation in another room, Martin said to me: 'David, that's who we're doing it for. It's the young people growing up around us. We owe it to them to make their future better.'

Gracie was usually a bit shy with strangers, so to see her so happily in Martin's arms was surprising to say the least. After he left, Joanne, Margaret and I talked about the way he'd bonded with Gracie. It seemed to us that she had recognised something inherently good in him.

By October 2010, with a financial package now in place and a construction company appointed to restore the church to its former glory, my attention immediately turned to the reopening and rededication of the building, which had not been used as a place of worship since 2002.

At First Derry, we wanted to celebrate and we wanted to share our jubilation not only with Protestant denominations and their clergy but also with the Catholic church and clergy. Very particularly we wanted to include Methodists, whose Carlisle Road church and halls we had been using, without restriction, since our own property had become unsafe.

But we also wanted to utilise this once-in-a-lifetime opportunity – and our location on the walls – for a citywide gesture of reconciliation. Accordingly, in our monthly congregational committee meetings, we considered inviting the Bloody Sunday families, whose loved ones had been killed by British paratroopers in Derry in January 1972, and the Claudy families, whose loved ones had perished in an IRA bomb in July of the same year. There is, as the Bible says, a time for everything under the sun and the reopening and rededication of a Presbyterian church in the heart of a Catholic–nationalist–republican city was surely the right time to think of doing things differently. We hoped that sowing some new seeds might allow the people of this divided city to begin living better together.

The plans to mark the reopening of the church soon gathered momentum. My ruling elders were not opposed to making this historic service both cross-community and inter-denominational. I was pleased by their willingness to not just invite the city's Catholic bishop, which by itself was a departure from the status quo, but to ask him to participate in the service.

Other ideas, in addition to involving other Protestant church representatives, included extending invitations to the NI First and deputy First Ministers, the PSNI Chief Constable, Derry City Council's Mayor, the Lord Lieutenant for the City of Londonderry, the American Consulate, the NI Assembly Speaker, the Enterprise, Trade & Investment Minister, as well as other local civic and political leaders.

During the planning, I suggested to the elders that someone representing our neighbouring communities of the Bogside, Brandywell and Creggan should be given a role in the service. This was nothing short of pushing the envelope along the table to see how far it might go – it could have been interpreted as me wanting to go too far too quickly. But, as the poet T.S. Eliot said, 'only those who will risk going too far can possibly find out how far one can go'.

During meetings with Martin, which quietly continued behind the scenes, I shared our plans for the service. Conscious of the price First Derry Presbyterians had paid during years of civil unrest, Martin was astonished by the congregation's willingness to be so forgiving and tolerant: 'David, your church is very special. Your people are showing all of us what we need to do.' These were sentiments he often reiterated when we were together.

'This service will catch the media's attention,' he told me. 'By being brave with your thinking and courageous about a different way of doing things, you will send out a very important message – that we don't need to be forever bound by the past.' The fact that Martin and I were regularly meeting up was, by itself, proof that neither of us wished to be imprisoned by the past.

Of course, there were those who appeared to derive pleasure in pouring cold water on my friendship with Martin by suggesting that the former IRA leader had charmed me into Sinn Féin's back pocket and that the whole thing was nothing more than one big publicity stunt for republicanism.

Others attempted to bring me down to earth with a thud by calling me naive for 'getting into bed' with a 'terrorist'. 'A leopard never changes its spots' was a remark I frequently heard from people who just couldn't stand – or for that matter understand – that Martin and I were friends.

Work continued to progress well at the church. However, the issue of final costs and a possible shortfall in government funding set alarm bells ringing. Before First Derry was brought under the umbrella of the Built Heritage Programme, a large sum of money had been expended by the Congregational Committee to prevent the church roof from collapsing. As a result, First Derry's own resources had been depleted. A letter from the NITB, the administrators of the funding, informed me that 'as the project has progressed there have been significant increases in costs leading to a shortfall in the funding available for this project; in order to meet this shortfall, the church may be required to increase its contribution.' I was worried.

Martin, in his influential position as NI's deputy First Minister, was the first and only person I thought of contacting. First Derry had already donated a massive £300,000 and any expectation of a further instalment from the church was unrealistic. Martin, who was always hands-on as far as First Derry's restoration was concerned, did not waste any time in raising his voice on our behalf at the highest level. In characteristic optimistic form, he assured me: 'David, I don't do problems; I only do solutions. Leave this one with me.'

Richard Moore, blinded by a rubber bullet in 1972, leads the
Carols on the Walls service.

5

Carols on the Walls

In the early years of my ministry, I wouldn't have considered driving through the Bogside. Over the last ten years or so, however, I've found myself driving there more and more to connect with Catholics, nationalists and republicans. Places such as Dove House, the Gasyard Centre, the House in the Wells (a refuge for men dealing with alcohol addiction), An Cultúrlann Uí Chanáin and the Museum of Free Derry began to invite me to events, and became places where I was warmly welcomed. My friendship with Martin had helped to break the ice and seemed to be widely appreciated.

In my opinion, in the figurative parlance of the Bible, we need to leave behind the dusty soils of Egypt and cross the Red Sea to reach the Promised Land. These visits to the Bogside were my way of moving out of my comfort zone to meet and to talk with people, but I never thought that my initial visit to the Gasyard community centre in 2010, which was by invitation, would lead to a Christmas initiative designed to bridge the gap between First Derry and the Catholic people of the Bogside. Our efforts at reaching out were being reciprocated.

At the coffee shop, I met some of the staff, and our common vision soon became clear: to identify something to catch the attention of people from all faith backgrounds and none, and to bring them together for an enjoyable event and shared experience.

Having a musician at the table encouraged us towards having a musical event involving church and school choirs. Songs have the power to mould and motivate. We decided on a cross-community, interfaith musical event. Nothing could have been more appealing with the festive season just around the corner.

Aware of how Derry's walls had effectively divided Catholics and Protestants in the past and kept them apart, we decided to use them as a place to unite different creeds and cultures. The plan entailed bringing diverse groups from around the city on to the walls to participate in a carol concert – Christmas is, after all, a time of year when virtually everyone is prepared to display some goodwill.

In the days leading up to the event, snow began to fall, until it lay 'deep and crisp and even'. We were worried the weather would deter people from attending. If anything, the snow added to the atmosphere – we could not have been more pleased by the community's response. The evening hadn't been straightforward to organise, but the rewards were great, as we discovered, with the large mixed crowd happily standing on the walls singing carols. For about an hour and a half, harmony reigned as the voices of children and adults rang out over the Bogside and beyond. All present heard, albeit briefly, the melodious music of peace.

We had hoped to attract some key civic and political figures, along with a cross section of citizens from both the Cityside and Waterside. All our expectations were exceeded – clergy, councillors, the local MP, MLAs, teachers, community leaders, children, teenagers, parents and grandparents were all there. The arrival of the deputy First Minister was greeted by applause. Shortly after the carol singing had ended, I went to find Martin, who was in the middle of the crowd, shaking hands and talking.

With Rev. Michael Canny and Richard Moore at the service.

Reaching into the pocket of his heavy dark-coloured overcoat, he handed me a gift. We shook hands and wished each other season's greetings.

The gift turned out to be a book of prayers suitable for both private and public use by Liam Lawton entitled *The Hope Prayer*. Opening the book, I discovered a handwritten message:

> David and Margaret,
> We wish you both a very Happy
> Christmas and Peaceful New Year.
>   In Hope
> Derry – Londonderry leads the
> way to a 'Bright Brand New Day'.
>   le gach dea ghuí
>   from
> your friends Martin & Bernie.

For as long as I've been a clergyman, I have always been on the lookout for fresh and thoughtful material to incorporate into my pulpit ministry. Ideas for sermons, children's talks and prayers have been the reason for my recurrent browsing of shelves in countless bookshops. Lawton's book of prayers, hammered out in the crucible of his own life-journey, was instantly riveting, primarily due to the substance of the content that appeared to encompass virtually every facet of human existence. Martin and Bernie had selected the perfect gift.

Martin's respect and thoughtfulness was distinctive and not only in the type of book he selected to give me. It was also conspicuous in the language he used in his inscription, which included both 'Londonderry', and 'best wishes' in Irish.

Martin's Christmas present has been well used. Prayers from Lawton's marvellous book have resounded from Presbyterian pulpits, effectively bridging the gap between heaven and earth and between the divine and the human. On occasions, I used some of the prayers to conclude meetings between Martin and myself.

Of all the items I have accumulated during my lifetime, nothing is more important to me than this book, personally signed by Martin, and given to me at the end of a unifying Christmas event on the walls of Derry-Londonderry.

The rededication of First Derry, May 2011.

6

First Derry Reopens

The more time I spent with Martin, the more I realised that he was a man who was changing – a fact that also became apparent to many of those who attended the memorable rededication service at First Derry on Saturday 14 May 2011.

The capacity congregation of almost seven hundred people was comprised of the widest possible cross section of people. On one side of the gallery sat the families of those killed on Bloody Sunday; directly opposite were relatives of those killed in the Claudy bombs of 1972. Elsewhere, throughout the church, Catholics sat alongside Protestants. Many from the neighbourhood from which bottles, bricks, stones and paint bombs had been launched at the church made their way to First Derry. What a spectacle – unity in diversity was clear for all to see. There were a number of people who came that day who didn't attend any church, let alone a Presbyterian one. A rainbow of creeds and cultures had converged on First Derry. The make-up of the congregation that day exceeded my wildest hopes, and was a prime example of what we should be striving to do in any divided society.

If the congregation was an amalgam of difference, the same was certainly true of the clergy officiating at the service. A procession of priests and ministers made their way to the front of the church. Never before had a non-conformist church, from the Presbyterian tradition in the north-west, reached out so far in an effort to be more inclusive. History was being made, and boundaries were gently being stretched, especially when the Catholic Bishop of Derry, Séamus Hegarty, was invited to the lectern to read from the Bible. Afterwards he told me that it had been the first time he had taken part in Protestant worship. We were attempting to do things differently, and our first small achievement was that no one stood up to object or walk out in protest – a great personal relief to me.

© Lorcan Doherty, PressEye

Preaching at the service.

While the reopening and rededication ceremony was conducted by the Moderator of the General Assembly, my elders nonetheless felt I should preach the sermon because of my local knowledge and the cross-community relationships I had developed. At the end of the sermon, which had the title 'Living Better Together', the entire congregation rose from their pews to applaud. That was the first time I had received a standing ovation for preaching a sermon. I was taken aback by the congregation's spontaneous reaction; I recall being emotional and taking a few moments to compose myself. Later, during refreshments in the Guildhall provided by Derry City Council, a visiting Church of England minister who had been sitting in the same pew as Martin, said to me, 'David, as soon as you finished your sermon, Martin McGuinness got to his feet and started clapping and everybody followed him.'

At the end of the religious service, the congregation was asked to take their seats again. There followed speeches from a range of people all keen to congratulate First Derry, to acknowledge the congregation's forbearance during nine years of displacement and to offer their good wishes for the future. The first speaker at the lectern was Martin. I introduced him to the congregation by saying, 'Ladies and gentlemen, sitting in church is a man I've got to know over the past five years. It all began in response to my radio appeal for help to bring an end to the paint-bomb attacks on our church. Please welcome my good friend, Martin McGuinness.'

© Lorcan Doherty, PressEye

Martin with PSNI Chief Constable Matt Baggott.

Martin kicked off by referring to his first meeting with me in the kitchen as the most expensive cup of tea he'd ever had because it led to First Derry receiving £1.6 million of government funding. He also spoke affectionately about his working relationship with Ian Paisley and how they had both decided that the time had come to look to the future. He revealed that Ian Paisley had been the first person to call him on the night in 2010 when the news broke that Derry/Londonderry had been awarded the UK City of Culture 2013 title. Martin said he'd been in Liverpool for the announcement and, as he was walking along the street, he heard his phone ring. It was Ian Paisley offering his heartiest congratulations to the city. What a story.

He also went out of his way to praise the people of First Derry for their willingness to reach out across the walls to include people from different backgrounds. While Martin was commending the congregation for their bravery and courage during difficult times, and stressing how important it was for the congregation to have their space respected and not attacked, I was glancing round the church to observe the body language of those whom I knew to be victims and survivors of IRA violence. A former IRA leader of Martin's stature was not only inside a Protestant church but he was speaking from the same area at the front of the church where, at different intervals over a handful of years, the coffins of five First Derry church members, all killed by the IRA, had rested. This was anything but easy for many sitting in the pews. I felt very anxious about how Martin would be received.

All eyes were focused on the man standing at the lectern and every ear was tuned in to his voice. Undeniably this was new territory for almost everyone in the church. Fortunately, there was no heckling. Everyone showed respect, even as Martin referred to the hurt and pain that had taken place during the conflict.

Standing outside the church after the service, I was bidding farewell to Martin, who was about to get into his ministerial car, when I saw a First Derry member whose brother had been murdered by the IRA approach us. He momentarily took my breath away; I didn't quite know what to expect. Amazingly, as the man got closer to where Martin and I were standing, he stretched out his hand towards Martin who stretched out his hand. As they shook hands, the member said, 'Martin, you spoke very well in church.' Astounded, I watched and listened as Martin expressed his appreciation, saying how much he'd enjoyed the service.

I was aware, though, that there was disquiet among some of the congregation about Martin's participation, especially from those who had lost family members in the Troubles. Although I was glad of my friendship with him, and grateful for his support, this in no way diminished my support and care for members of First Derry who had experienced first-hand the full impact of the IRA campaign in the city.

One lady, who had been sitting diagonally behind Martin during the service, had been with her father, a part-time RUC reservist, when he was murdered by an IRA gunman as they walked to church. The last person on earth she wanted to either listen to or see in her church was Martin McGuinness.

A few days after the reopening, I called at her home to hear her story. For more than two hours I listened spellbound as she told me the story of how her daddy was murdered in the street outside Claremont Presbyterian Church. (Claremont amalgamated with First Derry in 1996.) It was as if it had all happened the previous day, such was the potency of this terrible tragedy. I greatly valued directly hearing this painful story from her. It helped me to understand a little more the personal pain, and the rawness of that pain, that, even after decades, has neither dissipated nor diminished.

Hearing these stories helped me see how completely divided our communities were. It was clear to me that the past would be repeated if we continued to live in isolation from each other. Conversations such as I had with some of my parishioners, as well as my neighbours across the walls, confirmed to me that if our children were to have a better future, people in both communities would need to meet, mix and learn to live together. In the words of Martin Luther King, Jr., 'We've learned to fly the air like birds, we've learned to swim the sea like fish ... and yet we haven't learned to walk the earth as brothers and sisters.'

Welcomed on to the stage by Martin at the 2011 Ard Fheis.

7

Ard Fheis

Life is laced with mystery. I had never expected that my 2007 appeal on Radio Foyle would have led to a friendship with Martin – but it did. We had become comfortable in each other's company and were on a similar wavelength, particularly when it came to grasping opportunities to stretch ourselves for the purpose of healing and reconciliation. It was this way of thinking that dominated many of our conversations, including our discussions around the 2011 Sinn Féin Ard Fheis and the invitation from Martin for me to address delegates, as keynote speaker, on the opening night.

Sinn Féin's decision to come north, to Belfast, for its party conference for the first time was a momentous one.

Given how strongly I felt about the importance of breaking down barriers and coming together, irrespective of our beliefs or religions, I agreed to speak. This was an opportunity for me to connect directly with republicans and, in a gentle, non-judgemental way, to share some aspects of the Protestant-unionist narrative. Martin discussed the Ard Fheis with me, explaining the running order and my place in it. Then he said, 'You can speak on whatever subject you wish. The platform is yours to share with us what you think we need to hear.'

I had around two weeks to compose my speech. It was anything but easy. Right up until the night before, I was writing and rewriting. Even though I was accustomed to public speaking and to regularly producing scripts for Sunday sermons, this assignment was by far the most complex and daunting of my life. In the Ard Fheis audience would be those who some unionists branded unreconstructed terrorists. Watching the event on TV would be the injured and bereaved. I prayed for the wisdom of Solomon as I sat tapping on the keyboard of my computer into the early hours.

My daily interaction with people living in Derry confirmed there was a need for hope. Looking around, I could see some were smiling, but their eyes were dead. Others talked, but the music had left their voices. So many were like mannequins; all dressed up and going nowhere because they were feeling hopeless. I felt I had a God-given opportunity to address an all-Ireland political party that might be able to bring about some semblance of change.

When word got out a couple of days in advance of the event that I would be guest speaker, the public reaction, not surprisingly, ranged from fulsome endorsement to outright disapproval. A few unionist politicians interviewed on radio said they would like to advise me on the content of my address while other commentators applauded my attendance, welcomed my bravery and wished me well.

The day of my speech arrived, 9 September 2011. Approaching the Waterfront Hall, where the event was taking place, I could see a large crowd gathered in circular formation. As I got closer, I saw Sinn Féin president Gerry Adams, Martin, MLAs Martina Anderson, Mitchel McLaughlin and Raymond McCartney, along with many other faces I recognised from television. Martin began walking towards me and greeted me with an outstretched hand, a broad smile and an embrace. His Sinn Féin colleagues welcomed me warmly too – I hadn't expected a reception like this. Hands to shake and words of welcome were coming from every possible angle. Cameras were clicking everywhere. I distinctly recall thinking to myself, these people have got the wrong guest list, because I was being treated as if I was the American president. Sinn Féin had rolled out the red carpet. This was a big moment for all of us and the media was out in force to capture it.

Arriving at the Ard Fheis.

The welcome continued inside the Waterfront. A dark-haired, wiry, slender man shook my hand and introduced himself as Declan Kearney, Sinn Féin national chairperson. I hadn't even heard of Declan before but, holding on to my hand, he said, 'David, this may seem like a strange word to use, but I'm for using it anyway because I mean it: it's lovely to have you with us this evening. You are very welcome.'

Declan and I have continued to meet since the Ard Fheis. Like Martin, Declan now comes to my home where, among other things, we appraise political progress, discuss ideas for defrosting relationships and examine how best to promote healing and reconciliation. This has helped us get to know each other better.

Chaperoned to the front row in the spacious conference hall, I was shown to my seat next to Gerry Adams, who made me feel very welcome. I proceeded to listen to a number of articulate young delegates, from different parts of Ireland, speak on various issues. After this, Martin was introduced as the first speaker of the evening session. He struck me as confident and completely at ease. His inspiring speech ended with the words: 'We have different allegiances but that's all right. We have one thing in common – we believe in peace, we believe in moving forward together, we believe in sharing.' While Martin was introducing me to the audience, I was nervously making my way onto the stage. He came to meet me and we both warmly embraced. Then, Gerry Adams, who, by now, was sitting on the platform, left his seat and came across to where Martin and I were standing. He shook my hand and we spontaneously embraced.

Walking across to the podium where I placed my notes, I remember looking at the packed audience and thinking, help. I was petrified. I was not in a Presbyterian pulpit; I was in a very different place. But regardless of how the audience was dressed, or what the slogans behind me said, I was speaking to people, made in the image of God.

As the pause before I spoke seemed to lengthen, it was time to share my message, nervous as I was. I said, 'How can I follow Martin McGuinness?' Then, turning towards him, I continued, 'Martin, I see you as one of the true great leaders of modern times.' The hall suddenly came alive with loud applause, cheering and whistles. These sentiments certainly resonated mightily with party delegates inside the Waterfront.

I hadn't planned to say this in advance – but my rationale for these words was based on Martin's successful partnership with Ian Paisley as they jointly ran Northern Ireland from Stormont; his brave denunciation of dissident republicans as 'traitors to the island of Ireland' after PSNI Constable Steven Carroll's murder; and also his fluency in public speaking, which I'd just witnessed.

The invitation to address an Ireland-wide republican gathering was both a privilege and a responsibility. I knew that many from the Protestant tradition were hoping I would make good use of my visit by pointing the finger of blame firmly in the direction of the people who they felt had brought Ulster to its knees. I chose not to travel down that particular road. Thirty years of preaching has taught me that the quickest way to lose your audience is to bombard them with criticism, dangle them over the flames and scold them for their sinfulness. I chose a gentler approach.

Once the applause had stopped, I began to speak. This, I believed, was a divinely appointed moment that could not be squandered. I attempted to draw attention to the way both sides, long locked into their respective comfort zones of isolation and poor relations, had miserably failed to understand each other or do anything about one another's grievances. The message I wanted to deliver to my attentive audience was that our divided society, like every other divided society, espouses different competing narratives. Whether or not it was what they wanted to hear, I was anxious for the gathering of Sinn Féin delegates to hear from my lips that we all fell into a maelstrom that had robbed families, regardless of their creed or culture, of valued loved ones and inflicted life-changing physical and psychological injuries. Standing in judgement of the 'other side' was a futile and pointless exercise as no one's hands are altogether clean and no one's heart is altogether pure.

Prior to the Ard Fheis, I had privately taken some soundings from different sections of society that had been directly affected by years of conflict. Everyone agreed that some expression of remorse from republicans would contribute to healing. It was my belief that a countrywide day for hope and transformation could be the catalyst to bring that about; for everyone involved in the conflict to come together to acknowledge the pain each had visited on the people of Northern Ireland. A willingness by all to admit that we had, to a lesser or greater extent, not only hurt each other but that we had been hurt by each other would somehow and, in some small way, facilitate the healing of hurts and the mending of minds. Accordingly, my Ard Fheis address inexorably moved towards the climax of a genuinely heartfelt appeal to republican delegates to help make this happen.

The audience stood as I finished speaking – there was sustained enthusiastic clapping and cheering, and that was pleasing. As I made my way towards the exit, I was repeatedly stopped by delegates wanting to shake my hand and to thank me for being with them.

As soon as I was in the foyer, the media descended. They asked many probing questions, particularly about my description of Martin as 'one of the true great leaders of modern times'. The adulation of the conference hall dissipated very quickly, and I was forced to defend my decision to attend and to explain my comments about Martin. It felt as though I had been lifted off a mountain and dropped into a valley. But I stuck to the message I had delivered.

On my way back to Derry the next morning, I stopped off in Antrim to buy a newspaper. I wanted to catch up with the range of reactions to Sinn Féin's first northern conference as well as to my visit and speech. Moving around the newspaper stand, I caught sight of a bold headline on the front page of the *News Letter*. It read, 'LATIMER WALKS ON VICTIMS' GRAVES.' I was stunned by these words. They were cruel and totally untrue.

The remainder of the journey home seemed to take longer than usual. While I knew I had the support of my family, I was worried about the reaction when I got back to Derry. I drove to the church hall where a fundraising event was taking place, at which I was expected. One of the first things I saw as I entered the hall was a copy of the newspaper with the damning headline sitting on one of the tables. Conversation in the hall was laboured; the mood, moreover, was heavy and that to me conveyed how people viewed my Ard Fheis visit and speech. The newspaper headline was very damaging.

Once I got back home, my thoughts turned to the next morning: the Royal Air Force Association was parading to First Derry for their annual remembrance service. I was dreading the very thought of going to church, let alone preaching a sermon. I lay on top of the bed, alone with my thoughts and in a complete muddle as to how I would handle the service the next morning. Around 8 o'clock the telephone rang. I didn't want to answer it, thinking it would be someone looking to give me a piece of their mind. Very reluctantly, I lifted the receiver. 'Is that the Reverend Latimer?' the caller enquired. When I confirmed it was, the caller continued, 'You don't know me, but earlier today I was in a garden centre coffee shop reading the *News Letter*.' I was sure I was about to be denounced for daring to mix with republicans. 'I felt I had to make contact with you. I found your number in a telephone directory. I'm glad to get speaking with you. I wanted you to know as I watched you on television last night embracing Martin McGuinness and Gerry Adams I thought, I am seeing an example of Christian living.' I informed this mysterious caller, who identified himself as a Methodist living in Coleraine, how I was not looking forward to conducting worship the next morning with RAF ex-servicemen on parade. 'I will pray for you,' he said, 'and ask God to give you words strong and true to share with your congregation in the morning.'

Next morning, I welcomed the Londonderry Branch of the RAF Association to worship in First Derry. Medals were jangling and standards were unfurled. When it came to the sermon, on the subject of victory, I followed my prepared script until I reached the third part, which I had called 'Heavenly Victory'. My script slipped out of sight but I did not stop speaking; my mouth was mysteriously filled with words. Effortlessly I continued preaching. Never before or since have I had such an experience. This was divine intervention, rendering an otherwise formidable human situation manageable and profitable.

As I made my way from the pulpit past the choir stalls, a man reached out to embrace me and said, 'David, if someone had done forty years ago what you are now doing, my brother might still be living.' Shaking hands with ex-service personnel as they left church, one of them whispered, 'Blessed are the peacemakers.'

The following day, I took part in a number of radio interviews. I was questioned about my attendance at the Ard Fheis and also about my approval and blandishment of a former IRA terrorist. To clarify, I turned to the Bible and to pivotal figures like Moses, King David and Saint Paul. None of these people were paragons of virtue. Quite the contrary. Each of them had a terrible and, at times, violent past. Yet none of them were dismissed, ignored or rejected by God. Far from it. All became exalted leaders and respected role models – which goes to prove that, from God's perspective, every weed is a potential rose and every sinner a potential saint.

The storm generated by my attendance at the Ard Fheis and the substance of my address soon subsided. The media attention was replaced by a torrent of emails, letters and telephone calls from individuals living in different parts of Northern Ireland and further afield. A representative sample of the correspondence reveals that one man's meat is indeed another man's poison.

'Thank you for attending the Sinn Féin gathering at the weekend. I do believe that what you did was right. Yes, you are right and difficult it may be but forgiveness is required on all sides.'

Coleraine, County Londonderry

'Congratulations on having the courage and the grace to forgive and to say sorry. If only our church would take this stand and move forward and cherish a time of toleration and peace and love.'

Belfast

'I hope you will forgive me for intruding on your busy life. I have been so impressed by your visit to the Sinn Féin conference last Friday. You received a well deserved warm welcome and delivered a fine address. I know you went in the strength of the Lord and a wall of prayer surrounding you.'

County Fermanagh

'A few months ago, I approached you with a request to speak at our church. You graciously consented to do so. In light of recent events in the Waterfront Hall, the public reaction and, bearing in mind that this area suffered considerably during The Troubles, it is with regret that we will have to call off your visit.'

County Tyrone

'As a life-long member of the Presbyterian Church in Ireland and an elder of long standing, I am abhorred at your support for Martin McGuinness of Sinn Féin/IRA who are inextricably linked. Have you no compassion or understanding for what the victims of republican terrorism have suffered? Do you realise the pain, hurt and anguish you are causing these victims' families? As a minister of the Christian faith, they feel you have abandoned them to support a former terrorist.'

County Tyrone

'As Protestants and as Presbyterians we are absolutely disgusted at your recent meeting with Martin McGuinness Sinn Féin IRA. As somebody who is personally affected by the murdering actions of the IRA, we find it absolutely appalling that a Protestant, never mind a minister, would shake hands and hug a leading member of Sinn Féin IRA. Personally, we think you should resign from the Presbyterian Church.'

County Down

'As a Presbyterian personally affected by the IRA bomb at the Cenotaph in Enniskillen, I feel "qualified" to offer my opinion on your behaviour recently. You were invited to speak as a Presbyterian minister and no doubt you were aware there would be some who did not agree. It is my opinion you should not have agreed to speak in the first place. It would appear that your friendship with Mr McGuinness was well used by Sinn Féin and, as usual, they gained everything from the evening and you gained nothing but notoriety.'

County Fermanagh

'My wife and I wish to thank you for your courage in addressing the Sinn Féin Ard Fheis last week. Thank you for the thoughtful content of your talk. I am sure most of the gathering expected a type of address reminding them of the murder and the mayhem which they and their friends in the IRA carried out over the past forty years. Instead, you totally disarmed them by addressing them as a Christian minister on love and forgiveness. It was brilliant.'

Derry

'As an active member of the Presbyterian Church, I was appalled at your behaviour, praising Martin McGuinness as one of the "true great leaders of modern time". Could you imagine the piercing hurt this would cause to members of both communities who were affected by IRA violence? Of course there needs to be reconciliation in Northern Ireland; of course there needs to be demonstrations of Christian love – if you would stick to these goals, you would indeed be well served.'

County Down

'I would like to applaud you for recent events and to say I understand the way you are doing all you can to try to show the people of this little country how to live. There are so many trying to divide and few of us who are trying to bring folk together. Let's hope that, bit by bit, little ventures to meet our brother man will have some good effect.'

County Tyrone

'Innocent victims watched in horror as you betrayed Christians by embracing an IRA Commander. You referred to this IRA Commander as a "true great leader of modern time". How disgraceful. This has been a massive insult to victims as it would appear you choose to walk on the graves of our loved family members who sacrificed their lives so that people like you could walk the streets freely today. To speak at such an event was insulting to all Presbyterians; the comments you contributed were appalling.'

County Armagh

'I heard you speaking on the media this week … and thought you were an inspiration. I am with you all the way and cannot help but admire your courage. You are assisting us to move into a new area by breaking new ground. Far from your being timid and tepid, I think you said things which had to be said and which will have to be accepted by Unionists.'

County Tyrone

'I listened with interest to your interview on radio this morning. Your Christian approach to the matter, your calm and inclusive manner, your language of peace and reconciliation and your ability to react to those who might seek to antagonise, leads me to one conclusion:

you are truly a blessed man.'

County Antrim

'For the next wee while, the road might be rough. Many in our Presbyterian Church will just keep their heads down. But in their hearts they know you're on the right road.'

County Tyrone

'I want to write to say how much I appreciated your words and actions with respect to how the two main communities here might reach out to each other, live alongside each other and forgive. Your words are prophetic and your actions humbling.'

Londonderry

'The question from me to you is: who gave you the right to tell Martin McGuinness he is "a true great leader of modern times". Your job is a minister for the Protestant people of Northern Ireland – not a politician or maybe you're an IRA sympathiser or maybe a priest in undercover. You, sir, have surrendered the whole Protestant Nation to the hands of a Republican Sinn Féin Quartermaster.'

Kilkeel, County Down

'I wish to congratulate you for the message of hope and reconciliation at the weekend. I hope "the day of peace" becomes a reality and I will pray for that every day. I commend your courage and bravery and I hope you have the health and strength to continue with this message.'

England

The last thing I wanted to do by attending the Ard Fheis was to intensify the hurt that had been inflicted by the IRA across three decades. Clearly those who were hurting were not ready to hear me endorse the former IRA commander-turned-peacemaker as a great leader. I was taken aback by the tone in many of the letters and emails. However, more than half of all the messages were overtly supportive and positive, and it was this that gave me wind for my sails to lift up my chin and to keep moving forward. You don't make peace by just talking to your friends.

The graffiti that appeared in the Fountain Estate after the Ard Fheis.

Martin, like me, was surprised by the graffiti that was painted onto a wall in the staunchly loyalist Fountain Estate soon after my address to Sinn Féin delegates. It read: 'Dads [sic] Army padre joins SF/IRA. Good bye, David!' Many voices, including Martin's, spoke out against this protest. I wasn't too upset or frightened by the Fountain message or the manner in which my service in Afghanistan had been portrayed but the Territorial army, an integral part of the British army, should never be described by anyone as Dad's Army. As far as I was concerned, the graffiti writers had shot themselves in the foot and made themselves look foolish. My family, initially shocked, were reassured in time that the threat against me should not be taken seriously, and moved confidently on, as I did too. I am very fortunate to have the unswerving support of Margaret and our family.

As a direct result of my speaking at the Ard Fheis, two families requested their disjunction certificates as they wanted to leave First Derry and transfer their membership to another Presbyterian congregation in the city. Somewhere in the region of twenty to twenty-five other families stopped attending. I know that they haven't joined another church – they simply don't want to occupy a pew for as long as I am the minister of First Derry. One middle-aged man, whom I visited after noticing he was absent from church, informed me that, while he didn't wish to attend First Derry because of my friendship with Martin McGuinness, he did want me to officiate at his funeral service when he dies.

No minister likes to have any reduction in attendance at Sunday worship. It is disappointing to see some empty spaces in church. Yet, I cannot speak highly enough of the forbearance and understanding of the majority of First Derry's members, who have stood alongside me, and who continue to give me their support, believing that what I am doing is right and for the greater good. The arrival of a few new young families has also been a source of encouragement.

Six miles across the Irish border in County Donegal, where I am also minister of Monreagh Presbyterian, no church members left following my appearance at the Ard Fheis. Quite the opposite – the congregation has increased in size. Their unqualified backing both for me as minister and my work in the community has been so reassuring.

For a few weeks after the Ard Fheis, I was stopped in the street every day by people from both traditions who wanted to shake my hand and say well done. On quite a number of occasions, taxi drivers pulled up alongside me either to jump out of their vehicle to shake my hand or roll down their car window to say a big thank you. That was something I did not expect to happen, but I'm glad it did because it kept me abreast of public feeling. I also noticed that people who previously would have stopped to speak to me, walked past. I understood that they were making their opinion known too.

People talk about making peace but often draw a line in the sand and say, 'I'll make peace here!' Peace, however, is going beyond where you want to go. It's about stepping out into the darkness and walking into the unknown. As the Protestant minister of a church on the edge of the Catholic Bogside, which had been battered and broken during the Troubles, the time came when I heeded a voice saying, 'Go out into the darkness.' In the words of poet Minnie Louise Haskin, 'I went forth and, finding the Hand of God, trod gladly into the night. And He led me towards the hills and the breaking of day.'

Chatting to Martin at Free Derry Corner at the launch of his Irish
presidential campaign.

8

Onwards and Upwards

Towards the end of September 2011 I was invited alongside other clergy and city figures to attend the official launch of Martin's campaign for the Irish presidency. My attendance at this Sinn Féin-organised event provoked a negative reaction in some quarters.

Just a month or so later, Radio Ulster's Sunday morning church service was broadcast from First Derry. Keen to make the congregation that day relatively representative of city life, I invited a range of public figures, including Martin, who travelled back the previous evening from campaigning in Roscommon to attend this service.

In my remarks at the beginning of the Radio Ulster service, I intentionally drew the attention of the listening audience to Martin being in the church and welcoming him as my very good friend. It was an indication of our growing friendship and of his commitment to peace building at a grass roots level that he should take time out from his frenetic electioneering schedule to join with his Presbyterian neighbours for worship. Thankfully, no one who disagreed with Martin McGuinness worshipping in First Derry staged any sort of protest.

Immediately after the service, everyone gathered in the nearby Tower Hotel where refreshments were being served. I introduced a small group of men to Martin. The conversation quickly turned to the presidential election.

Martin was the centre of attention as he told us about the meetings he was addressing and the miles he was travelling. As Martin prepared to move further around the room, a prominent Protestant businessman within this small group spontaneously made a comment that is etched onto my memory. 'Martin,' he said. 'I hope you don't get elected because there's nobody ready to take your place.' Martin smiled before he continued making his way around the room, in which it was apparent that he was being welcomed, and where his attendance was appreciated.

After leaving the hotel, Martin and I made our way back round to the church and up to the minister's room for a pre-arranged short meeting to continue discussing how people, who had lost loved ones during the Troubles and are unable to forgive, could be brought – in the language of John O'Donohue – 'out of the anonymity of distance into the intimacy of belonging'.

These people needed a lifeline to bring them in from the cold. Sitting together in First Derry, I summoned up the courage to introduce an idea to Martin that had been fermenting for some time in my mind. Martin's paramilitary past and the pivotal role he played as an IRA commander for many years naturally led those who lost loved ones during the Troubles to see him very differently to the way I did. It was my belief that until people could see him differently the peace process would remain fragile. My idea was for republicans to issue a statement or acknowledgement similar to the one made by loyalist paramilitaries in 1994 – 'In all sincerity, we offer to the loved ones of all innocent victims over the past twenty-five years abject and true remorse.'

In my preparation for flying this kite to Martin, I had scribbled some thoughts on a piece of paper. I thought we could explore this idea of a public statement from the republican movement – a statement that, I believed, would pave the way to the snow melting and trust emerging between politicians. For a while, Martin and I examined how such a statement might look and what it should include. At the close of our meandering discussions, Martin asked me to write down what I thought should be in the statement with the plan that we'd meet again to discuss it after the election.

Soon after the presidential election, which was won by Michael D. Higgins, Martin and I got together once more, this time to select key phrases for a proposed public statement that might offer all hurting families a salve for their wounds. To facilitate our discussion, I produced the wording that I had agreed to write at our earlier meeting. Sitting opposite Martin, I began reading it:

'None of us sowed the seeds of enmity and division that have long characterised this part of Ireland. We inherited the mistrust, sectarianism, and separateness from previous generations of our own families that regrettably culminated in thirty years of conflict. The establishment of a devolved administration at Stormont is not a panacea. Something else is needed to soothe people's suffering and drive away their tears. For my part, I am prepared to show leadership by expressing genuine remorse to all whose hearts are breaking. My heart goes out to everyone who lost loved ones during the conflict. Together we can plant the shoots of reconciliation and work to bring about a better future for everyone, regardless of their creed or culture.'

Again, we batted ideas across the table as to the final shape of any statement and the value it would have in the community. I knew and admitted that there would be members of the Protestant/unionist/loyalist family who would dismiss any statement, regardless of its content, as a gimmick. A hallmark of our conversations was that we were honest with each other – this was vital if we were going to make progress in our discussions and advance the cause of understanding between our two traditions.

I offered to make First Derry church available for a press conference at which a statement could be delivered to the media. My rationale was that using a sacred space as the place from which to deliver the statement would reinforce the spirit of forgiveness and reconciliation at the heart of the statement and encourage a more ready acceptance from the Protestant and unionist communities.

Of course I was aware that while Martin was prepared to discuss this kind of statement with me, there would be many others within republicanism opposed to it. I was well aware that the wording of any statement would have to go through countless stages before seeing the light of day. Achieving consensus, we agreed, might even elude us.

To me, words are similar to seeds in that they don't take root immediately. They need time to germinate. Even talking about so sensitive a subject was tantamount to tilling the ground. At the time we first met, I could never have envisaged participating in conversations as serious and sensitive with him.

That no public statement of this sort was ever delivered could be perceived as a failure. But I'm not so sure. The record of the human race confirms that failure is never fatal. A quote from Winston Churchill helps, I think, with this perspective: 'I've never failed at anything in my life,' he once said. 'I was simply given another opportunity to get it right.'

I always believed that Martin was capable of confounding everyone, and taking the path less travelled. A statement didn't seem a million miles away, especially when I saw the moment of history that unfolded the following year.

Martin shakes hands with the Queen.

Martin had mentioned to me some time before it happened that he might be meeting the Queen. I ventured to suggest that he could not do anything other than shake her hand when they met if momentum in peace building across the country was to be maintained.

For Martin, the enormity of this event cannot be overstated. I struggled a little to empathise and told him, 'We will slip back if it doesn't happen and risk losing the gains we've made.' I believed that those who had suffered bereavement and injury during the Troubles, especially those from the unionist community, would take solace from seeing their monarch shake Martin's hand. This, I told Martin, could – in the fullness of time – help to breach the banks of the river of hurt in which so many were trapped.

When future generations come to study the history of these islands, I have no doubt that this historic handshake will feature prominently – a seismic step taken by a queen and a paramilitary-turned-peacemaker, who was determined that his ceiling could become the floor for those coming after him. In the words of Alfred Tennyson,

> I can but trust that good shall fall
> At last – far off – at last, to all,
> And every winter change to spring.

With Margaret at the celebrations to mark twenty-five years of ministry at First Derry.

9

Marking Twenty-five Years of Ministry

Change is one of life's certainties. Nothing stays the same forever, which is how it has been during my time as pastor and preacher at First Derry. I well remember seeing the building for the very first time in 1988, parcelled tightly in wire fencing and sealed securely with steel doors. As the years have passed, the building has been restored into an elegant eye-catching piece of built heritage, exuding simple architectural grandeur.

Change, however, is not peculiar to property – people also change. Back when I accepted the congregation's invitation to become their twenty-first minister, no one from First Derry would ever have gone to the Bogside, and the very thought of Martin McGuinness standing on the church's front steps – let alone being invited inside – would have been anathema to the entire congregation.

When the music changes, as it inevitably does with the passage of time, it can be a signal to start learning some new dance steps, otherwise you end up sitting on the sidelines.

The people of First Derry were unquestionably the right people in the right place at the right time. With some exceptions, the congregation were supportive of me seeking to turn a wall into a bridge and foster good relationships with our neighbours.

A snippet from one of John O'Donohue's poems sums up what was taking place in Derry. 'Somewhere, out at the edges, the night/Is turning and the waves of darkness/ Begin to brighten the shores of dawn.' Had this not been the case, reaching into the Bogside would not have been tolerated by my Presbyterian flock. One tiny step, followed by other tiny steps, across to the other side of the walls, laid the foundation for acceptance. This resulted in the last person anyone would have wanted to see in First Derry – namely Martin – regularly visiting.

One of these visits was a special Christmas carol service, which concluded with a choir heartily singing 'O Holy Night'. As he was leaving the church, he was on a high as he told me, 'That's my all-time favourite carol. You've made my Christmas.'

Easter 2013 marked twenty-five years since I had arrived at First Derry and Monreagh. Both congregations very kindly arranged special services to mark this milestone.

Spending twenty-five years in the same place is quite unusual for Presbyterian ministers. Most ministers choose to move around rather than remain at the one church. I have never felt inclined to move from First Derry and Monreagh, and when I reflect on the generosity of the people I have been privileged to serve for many years, I am completely satisfied with my decision.

The service at First Derry was the normal weekly Sunday morning service, enhanced by special music and singing from the church choir, and followed by a sumptuous lunch provided by the ladies of the congregation in the church hall. It is customary for a minister to invite family and friends to this kind of event, and included in my list of guests were the mayor of Derry, at that time Kevin Campbell, and the deputy First Minister. I chose to invite the mayor because of the support given to First Derry by the city council during our years of displacement, and Martin because of our close friendship. Both Kevin and Martin had attended the church previously so there was nothing too unusual about them being present, until after the benediction when there were a few speeches followed by the presentation of incredibly generous gifts to both Margaret and myself.

When it came to the mayor's turn to speak, the microphone at the lectern suddenly malfunctioned. In common with very many Presbyterian churches, First Derry has a lectern, from which people give the bible readings, and a pulpit, from where the minister preaches. To ensure everyone would hear Kevin speaking, I had no choice but to bring him up to the pulpit – the microphone there was still working. As the speeches were nearing an end, I went across to Martin, who was sitting close to the front of the church, and whispered in his ear, 'I think you're going to have to come to the pulpit.' Purposely, I had left Martin to the last. He came up the steps and into the elevated spacious pulpit, normally the privileged place reserved for ministers. While Martin was speaking, I was sitting across from him in one of the pulpit wings casting my eyes around the church. The pulpit was hallowed ground; how would the congregation react to having Martin McGuinness there? A few minutes into his speech there was a bright flash – someone had taken a photograph. Martin just kept on speaking – he didn't hesitate. Later that evening a member of the congregation rang me to say that a picture of Martin standing in First Derry's pulpit had appeared on Facebook along with the caption 'not in my name'. It was clear that not everyone had been happy about Martin's presence in the pulpit but, not for the first time, I felt relieved that at least no one had walked out.

During his 'pulpit' speech, which was unscripted, Martin referred to the courage displayed by First Derry; he praised the congregation for persevering during times of great difficulty. He went on to speak empathetically about the victims of the Troubles: 'I'm aware this church lost RUC and UDR members during the conflict. Today, in your church, which I love visiting, I offer you my heartfelt sympathy. I'm passionate about building a better future for all our families and especially for our children.' He also referred to meeting the Queen, praising her for participating in their joint gesture of peace building. His speech, which attracted applause, finished with him saying, 'God bless,' two words he frequently used at the end of a conversation or a visit.

A week or so after that service, a gentleman who had personally been impacted by the Troubles, made a point of telling me, 'David, I'm not so sure about Martin being in our pulpit, but what he said and the way he said it made his visit to First Derry worthwhile for me. I heard words I've been waiting to hear for years.'

A week later, another service – on this occasion in the afternoon – was arranged at the church in Monreagh. There was a happy and huge congregation, including members and ministers from neighbouring churches. A special feature of the service was the enthusiastic singing of old favourite metrical psalms and hymns. A great country afternoon tea in the old school house followed the service. A carnival atmosphere prevailed throughout the entire afternoon's proceedings, and no one was in any hurry to leave.

Proudly on show in our home are two particularly special and treasured gifts – one being a Comitti of London pendulum strike and chime wall clock presented by the congregation of

First Derry; the other a specially-commissioned Pat Cowley oil painting of Monreagh Presbyterian church, presented by the congregation of Monreagh.

With Mary McAleese at one of the 'Conversations Across Walls and Borders' events.

10

Son of the Dreamer

Two main themes dominated the conversations Martin and I had. One was exploring ways in which hearts broken by the torment of the Troubles might be mended; and the other was to investigate how young people, growing up across our city and beyond, could become partners in peace building.

Frustrated by the slow pace of change at Stormont, Martin would often remark, 'We politicians can't do this by ourselves; we haven't all the answers. We need everybody working together with us to make things happen.' And, on occasions, it was specifically the young he was thinking of who, unlike their parents and grandparents, were not encumbered by the tortuous baggage of the past and who are sometimes ignored simply because of their youth.

The success of the reopening service at the church had sowed the seeds in my mind that the church could provide a safe space for people living in a divided city to be together. I started to share my thoughts with people around the city to confirm that this was something worth pursuing. An initiative entitled 'Conversations Across Walls and Borders' emerged in the following weeks and months. The concept was to offer people from both sides of the river the opportunity to hear high-profile speakers articulate ideas for coexisting peacefully. The events were advertised widely, with great support from local media. Large cross-community audiences gathered to listen to Irish President Mary McAleese, international journalist Fergal Keane, PSNI Chief Constable Matt Baggott, and campaigner Richard Moore, who appeared with the British soldier who fired the plastic bullet that blinded him.

Speaking to students at the University of Cape Town in 1966, Robert Kennedy said, 'It's a revolutionary world that we live in and thus ... it is young people who must take the lead.' Empowering young people, who aspire for a cross-community togetherness of spirit, is the driving force behind this initiative. Governments can lay foundations but it is the young who will take the dream forward.

We invited schools and colleges to participate at each of these and other similar events. The energy, enthusiasm and excitement of the young people, from Protestant, Catholic and integrated schools, easily mixing together, was truly inspiring and most refreshing. Thanks to the city's Unity of Purpose Group, I was fortunate enough to meet a senior educationalist from the former Western Education and Library Board (WELB) who could see the value of the young people's participation in peace building.

Encouraged by the interest and support of the WELB, I shared with Martin how we planned to involve young people in schools in our initiative, which came to be called 'Pathway to Peace'. When Martin arrived at my home on one particular visit, he was welcomed by flip-chart sheets, scattered across the living room floor, mapping out a plan and timeline for involving pupils as peace builders. I can still see his face light up as I unwrapped details of this bespoke concept, designed expressly to reach out to as many children and young people as possible.

He smiled and said: 'David, I am one hundred and ten percent behind this initiative. I will do everything I can and help you in every way I can.' After Martin left, I was on cloud nine. To have support at that level was invaluable.

Subsequently, the WELB sent letters explaining the initiative to every school principal within the Derry City Council area to gauge support for this youth-led peace initiative. Amazingly, all fifty-six principals in the council area – embracing primary and post-primary schools in the controlled, maintained, integrated, Irish medium and special sectors – readily consented to participate. Every school/college was subsequently invited to create a twenty-five-word 'Peace Pledge' – an expression of what young people consider we all must do if we are to live better together. The peace pledge messages were later embossed onto ceramic tiles and arranged around the peace flame in a special garden that has become known as the Peace Garden, provided by Derry City Council.

The Peace Garden next to the Guildhall.

The energy and inspiration of principals, teachers and pupils led to further discussion about young people and the greater role they could play in peace building. At the time, I was thinking more and more about how we could make the most of Derry's year as City of Culture. The twelve-month programme of events was all about creating a new image for the city of Derry-Londonderry; an attempt to forge a new shared identity and promote a new understanding. It occurred to me that bringing young people – shimmering with fresh ideas, clear perspectives and positive energy – centre-stage was a no-brainer.

By their active involvement in Pathway to Peace, schools were nurturing young people as peacemakers. We were keen to give young people, growing up in emerging peace, a platform to raise their voices and share their vision for the future. I began to discuss the possibility of a large-scale event with a local steering group. We identified Guildhall Square as our preferred venue, and began to think about a speaker. Around that time, I saw Martin Luther King III, son of the dreamer, on television and, learning more about him, concluded he could be the person we needed most to help us move forward.

Connecting with the appropriate person at the King Foundation in America, however, was proving difficult. Martin came to the rescue by quickly putting me in touch with the Northern Ireland Bureau in Washington, whose director arranged a meeting between Martin Luther King III and me in Washington DC in mid-January 2013. By the close of our breakfast meeting, we had our key speaker. I felt like I was walking on air.

Welcoming Martin Luther King III to First Derry.

11

'He has a good heart, he's a good man'

A few months later, I met Martin Luther King III and his two travelling companions, Benetta (Beni) Qua Ivey and Jim Gaffey, who were close friends of the King family, as they stepped into the arrivals hall at Belfast International Airport on Friday 17 May 2013. I felt deeply thankful that they had made the journey. After a brief stopover at a hotel, we travelled to Stormont Castle to meet Martin and Peter Robinson, then First Minister. After walking on to the grass in front of the castle for a relaxed photo-shoot, we were taken inside to the First Minister's office.

The conversation, which extended for an hour, was cordial and friendly. Mr King used the opportunity to commend both men for the NI peace progress and their role in it. He also described Northern Ireland as a template of what is possible when enemies become partners. I recall him imploring both men to keep moving steadfastly forward to win the prize.

Both Martin and Peter freely talked about their good working relationship despite their constitutional and other differences. Their convivial body language and easy interaction with each other was pleasing to observe. Northern Ireland was changing for the better, Peter Robinson told King, but there was still a long way to go.

For his part, Martin quite openly remarked that, in the past, he and Peter wouldn't even have sat at the same table as one another. 'Peter and I are very different,' he said to King, 'but this in no way stops us working together. In fact, it makes both of us all the more determined to do everything we can to make this place better and brighter for all our citizens.'

Travelling to Derry from Stormont, as we talked in the car, it became clear that Martin Luther King III, Beni and Jim had been greatly impressed by the welcome they had received from both Peter and Martin at Stormont. Their visit to Northern Ireland had certainly got off to a great start. Somewhere around the Glenshane pass, Beni – who had been a confidante of Coretta Scott King and who was known in the King family for being a good judge of character – announced from the back seat of the car: 'David, I got a great feeling about Martin McGuinness during our meeting at Stormont; there's something about that man. I was watching him closely and I was listening to him carefully. That man has a good heart. He's a good man.'

Turning around from my front seat I said, 'I'd love you to tell Martin that directly when you meet with him on Sunday afternoon. He needs to be encouraged in the job he's doing.'

There was a programme of events over the weekend, including a public rally, to enable as many people as possible to meet Martin Luther King III, and for him to see the city, and to meet our own city's Nobel Peace Laureate, John Hume.

The King party was staying at the City Hotel, so on the day of the big rally, Sunday 19 May 2013, we'd asked political figures and members of the steering group to gather there before the event. I said to Martin that Beni had something to tell him. Without hesitation, she repeated to Martin exactly what she'd said in the car. He was filled with gratitude.

I was a little apprehensive about the day so stood still, apart from the conversations, looking out of the window. I was relieved and delighted to see crowds of people walking across the Peace Bridge in the direction of Guildhall Square.

When we arrived, our hopes for a big turnout were realised as more than six thousand people had crowded into Guildhall Square for the rally. It was a spectacular scene. Pupils, all attired in their different coloured uniforms, were omnipresent in the vast gathering of people. The sky was blue and the sun was shining. There was a great buzz with happy, smiling faces everywhere. During the afternoon event, designed to showcase the ability and expertise resident in our schools, pupils proudly read aloud their peace pledges before presenting them to Martin Luther King III.

In the midst of the crowd, with Martin and Martin Luther King III – thankful for such a big turnout.

A key part of the event was an act of acknowledgement – a pledge that everyone at the event would say together to express the pain that the Troubles had visited on the city, and to promise to live better together in the future. The wording of this was extremely sensitive so, over the period of a few months, I visited a wide cross section of different people, including trustees of the RUC George Cross Association, the Orange Order Grand Secretary, the PSNI Chief Constable, politicians, priests, ministers and business people, to seek their advice. The final statement, agreed just days prior to the event, was displayed on screens around Guildhall Square. Everyone present was invited to hold hands and say together:

> Mindful of our brief time on earth, it is with a sense of sadness we recall the grief-stricken experiences of thousands of people from our community occasioned by violent conflict. While bowing to the past, yet refusing to be bound by the past, it is the prospect of the future, which is ours to shape, that beckons us now. Therefore, we pledge ourselves to ensure this will never happen again as we turn our eyes towards the dawn of a new day.

In the presence of none other than Martin Luther King III, we had publicly pledged to do everything we could to make sure the future would be different to the past.

Woven into our act of acknowledgement were some of the words used by Queen Elizabeth II and by Mary McAleese at a state dinner in Dublin Castle in May 2011. Martin was pleased about this. On more than one occasion he had said to me, 'David, what Queen Elizabeth said in Dublin was groundbreaking. She has shown us all what we need to do. We're only at our strongest when we come together.'

As a truly great event concluded and the crowds gradually dispersed, the deep desire of a city, longing for change, could be summed up in words spoken by the great dreamer himself when he said, 'If you can't fly, then run; if you can't run, then walk; if you can't walk, then crawl; but, whatever you do, you have to keep moving forward.'

Martin with Angus Buchan.

12

Inspiration in a South Derry Coffee Shop

In the spring of 2014, I received a telephone call from a man who had recently been in the city for a day trip, which included a walk around the walls and a guided tour of First Derry. This stranger then shared a little bit of his life story. He lived in Magherafelt, south Derry, where he had his own business. He was a lead member of an independent Christian fellowship and passionately wanted people whose lives had been affected by years of conflict to experience healing and reconciliation.

To help bring this about, he and a small group of like-minded people had formed an organisation called Healing the Land. They had invited a man called Angus Buchan – a South African farmer, Christian leader, author and evangelist – to take part in a number of public religious rallies in the district. Although controversial, Buchan is renowned as powerful speaker. By choosing not to hold these rallies inside a church building, the organisers believed they could more effectively reach out to the entire community and, thereby, bring both Catholics and Protestants into the same space to listen to Buchan as he spoke about his personal experience of conflict and peace in South Africa.

The organisers wanted to extend an invitation to

Martin to attend one of the evening rallies but didn't know how to go about getting in touch. Aware of my friendship with him, they contacted me.

I was happy to help but I was keen to meet the committee and listen to their ideas and plans before I spoke to Martin himself. I also wanted to find out why they wanted him to attend.

A week or so later, I met them in a coffee shop in Castledawson. From the outset it was clear that this group was sincere about their intentions to convene two special rallies. A great many people in south Derry had suffered during the Troubles. Many had been physically hurt; others were psychologically scarred. Few were finding it easy to move forward. It was the organising committee's view that Angus Buchan, with his first-hand experience of inter-communal strife in South Africa and his track record of promoting healing and hope, could be the person to drive away the mists of despair and doubt and enable hurting families to catch sight of a way forward. This was commendable. I was fully supportive.

As for Martin, the organisers believed that his personal identification with their initiative would contribute to kick-starting a countrywide healing process. Although the organisers had deep reservations about Martin because of his IRA past they were, however, keen to learn more about the different path he appeared to be on. They were anxious to hear if it was genuine and they believed something good could emerge from bringing Martin McGuinness and Angus Buchan together.

Before leaving the meeting, one of the group said a prayer and, in his prayer, made specific reference to Martin McGuinness, even going as far as to ask for God's blessing on his life. Protestants praying for Martin McGuinness by name. I hadn't heard that happen before.

I rang Martin about the event and suggested it might be preferable for him to meet privately with Angus Buchan after one of the evening rallies rather than attend the event itself. Martin was happy either way.

In the end, Martin met Angus one evening in a Castledawson coffee shop. He had been at a meeting of the British-Irish Council in the Channel Islands but arrived into Belfast's George Best Airport shortly after 9 p.m. and was happy to stop off on his way home to Derry for the meeting.

A group of seven or eight men, including me and Angus Buchan, arrived at the coffee shop at around 9.45 p.m. While I was chatting to Angus, Martin telephoned to let me know he was on the motorway and wouldn't be much longer. When I passed on this information to the group, their conversation stopped. Silence filled the coffee shop. Everyone was nervous and had no idea what to expect.

'Angus,' I said, 'Martin is Catholic and will not be familiar with our Protestant evangelical language. Please go easy on him; we're wanting to open doors tonight – not close them.'

I then went out on to the street to wait. Soon, Martin's car pulled up and he quickly got out from the front seat and greeted me with a hug. I ran through who was inside.

'They're all nervous,' I told him.

'Let's meet them', he said. 'It can't be that bad.'

Confidently, he entered the coffee shop and made his way to the seated area where the group was waiting. No one was talking; to begin with no one moved. In spite of the group's keenness to meet Martin, this was clearly a leap into the unknown. Their nervousness was palpable. Martin approached each person in the group with an outstretched hand. Everyone in the group returned the gesture.

My greatest fear was that someone in the group might seize being in Martin's company as an opportunity to apportion blame for our country's pain or pronounce a harsh judgement. With no precise agenda for our informal encounter, I decided to speak first by welcoming Martin. I continued by outlining how the two of us had met, seven years previously.

The group, I observed, was listening intently. Turning to Martin, I invited him to speak. In his typically relaxed and down-to-earth style, he started by telling the group, as he removed his jacket, how happy he was to have crossed my path and how pleased he was that we had become good friends.

'Two very different people had been brought together,' he said, 'and our shared goal is to leave the world a better place for our children and grandchildren.' He went on to speak of his remarkable relationship with Ian Paisley and how the two of them had come together. 'I count Ian Paisley as one of my true friends,' he told the group. He went on to speak favourably of his partnership in government with First Minister Peter Robinson. He ended by talking about the day he shook hands with Queen Elizabeth and how that was necessarily preceded by him travelling around Ireland discussing this groundbreaking moment of reconciliation with Sinn Féin supporters, seeking to garner their support.

Something was happening around our table. No one was drinking; everyone was captivated by Martin's words. When Martin finished speaking, Angus Buchan, sitting across the table from Martin, began by commending Martin for his peace-building work, which he described as courageous, significant and timely. 'Northern Ireland, like South Africa, has been in a bad place, but God in His wisdom raises up leaders to point the way towards a better and different path. Martin, you are one of those leaders; may God keep your hand fixed to the plough and may you never look back.'

Angus prayed for Martin and for Peter Robinson, everyone at Stormont and the peace process. His words were carefully chosen. He entreated the Almighty to make Martin's endeavours enduring, finishing with a request for protection on Martin, his wife and family. Angus's words resonated with the entire group, and he used language that was inclusive and laced with generosity and grace.

Political and religious differences momentarily evaporated. It seemed to me that God was with us in the coffee shop, and evidence of this was clear by the way in which everyone said goodbye to Martin – his leaving was marked by warm handshaking and hugging. I watched, scarcely able to believe what I was seeing. The change in atmosphere was extraordinary.

At the coffee shop door, Martin and I stood alone. When I thanked Martin for fitting the meeting into his busy day, he replied, 'This has been the most important thing I've done all week.'

Back in the coffee shop, the group was flabbergasted by the way the meeting had gone. It would be an understatement to say that everyone present, in differing ways, had been moved by the experience. All the group had been greatly impressed by Martin's friendliness, openness and passion for peace. 'That man is a transformed man' was the consensus. Before going our separate ways, one of the group said that, had he not personally met Martin and listened to his story, he never would have believed such change was possible in any human being.

I made a point of telling Angus that I thought his

prayer was an inspiring component of the meeting. His response was: 'Reverend, tonight's meeting with Martin McGuinness in this coffee shop has made my visit to Ireland worth it all. I will remember and treasure this for the rest of my life.'

The unveiling of The Peace Pledge Tree at the
Amazing the Space event.

13

Amazing the Space

Following the success of the peace pledge initiative in our local schools, the programme extended across the three counties of the WELB area: from Drumsurn in the north-east to Derrylin in the south-west. In all, 230 schools – including schools in the border counties of Cavan, Donegal and Monaghan – each produced a twenty-five-word peace pledge. This youth-led peace-building initiative was now both cross-border and cross-community.

Keen to give the project even greater impact, I met representatives from Guinness World Records, who advised me that we had a good chance of setting a new world record within their category, Most Signatures on a Scroll. A large roll of fabric, kindly donated by Hunter Apparel Solutions in Derry, was conveyed from one WELB school to another by board maintenance staff, enabling sixty thousand children and young people to personally pledge peace for their country by signing their names on the scroll. We anticipate the announcement of our successful world record soon!

I continued visiting schools in other parts of Northern Ireland, introducing the initiative to principals, vice-principals and teachers, inviting their participation. In the end, a grand total of 409 schools throughout the province of Ulster participated by writing a peace pledge. As one school principal put it, 'Every school is glad to play their role and delighted to have an opportunity to share in this memorable programme to help mould and shape peace at grassroots level.'

Having embarked on a journey with young people and feeling overwhelmed by the results reflected in the inspirational words and wisdom woven into every school pledge, I now wanted to provide the young with a prominent platform on which they could come together for a countrywide gathering to shine a new light on the path and be the bridging narrative for the future.

At one of my meetings with Martin, which lasted for more than two hours, we discussed this proposed gathering. I had Maze Long Kesh in mind for a possible venue, my logic being that it was one of the many scarred spaces we have that in the past were identified with conflict. It was time to seize spaces like these for peace, and the people best placed to help with doing that were growing up in our cities, towns and villages. The successful use of this space by the Balmoral Show organisers confirmed the venue's suitability. Martin was supportive, and offered there and then to have his office arrange a meeting with the CEO of the Maze Long Kesh Development Corporation (MLKDC).

The first meeting at Maze Long Kesh was both illuminating and informative. Seeing is believing. I was impressed by the site's scale, but the surviving buildings also reminded me of its horrific past. Although it was barren and bleak, I could visualise it being invaded by hundreds of young people seeking to build bridges of understanding and reconciliation so that there would be no more harm done or hatred sown. I was convinced Maze Long Kesh was the right place for young people to make an impact and catch the public's attention, although very aware that making it happen there would not be easy. As it turned out, Martin's support for the event was pivotal.

The organisation of an event on this scale was a daunting prospect so I was delighted to be introduced to Co-operation Ireland by the MLKDC board chairman. Co-operation Ireland joined the Derry-based steering group as lead partner. The steering group, comprising teachers, performing arts personnel, a local sculptor and a community relations officer, also included an impressive cohort of very committed post-primary school students who have been 'hands on' in terms of design, development, leadership and promotion.

When I told Martin of the students' involvement, he remarked to me, 'Who better to map out a way forward than all the young people writing peace pledges? Our young people are not bogged down like we are, David. They've got clearer vision than us. We've got to give them a chance and make this thing work.'

A second visit to Maze Long Kesh was set up for the steering group members. As our visit was coming to an end, all were unanimous in our decision that the former jail space was the ideal venue. Returning home in the minibus, we discussed at length a name for this countrywide youth gathering. By the time we reached the outskirts of Derry, we'd arrived at the name 'Amazing the Space'. We felt that this play on words, that referenced both the venue's name and John Newton's famous hymn, gave a good sense of what we were trying to achieve: to transform a scarred place, and to claim it for peace.

There were hurdles to clear – such as funding, achieving cross-party support, and the logistics of bringing so many people from so many different schools to the one place – so Martin offered the support of his office, which was invaluable.

The peace pledges, created by pupils in schools around the nine counties of Ulster, formed the foundations of Amazing the Space. The decision by councils in Derry-Londonderry, Limavady, Omagh and Enniskillen to introduce permanent public displays of peace pledges led us to push for a permanent installation that would bring together all the peace pledges from the participating schools. This took the form of a fifteen-foot-tall galvanised metal tree incorporating hundreds of large metal oak leaves each embossed with a pledge.

Months of intensive activity culminated in more than three thousand pupils from schools in Northern Ireland and the border counties pouring into the Eikon Exhibition Centre, at Maze Long Kesh, to mark International Peace Day on Wednesday 21 September 2016. The key aim of the event was to give as big a platform and as loud a voice as possible to the young people's pledges. The sheer multiplicity of cross-community voices crying out for peace proved to be a happy thunder of voices none could ignore. The glittering highlight of the event – which included a panoply of performance, art and music by a myriad of talented young people, all in their different uniforms – was the unveiling of The Peace Pledge Tree, a truly spectacular piece of public art.

Towards the close of the event, the deputy First Minister was invited to the podium to read his twenty-five-word peace pledge, which he had readily agreed to write. Looking out over a sea of young faces he first congratulated the young for their outstanding displays and then continued by saying, 'I pledge to work tirelessly with everyone to ensure tolerance, equality and mutual respect become the bedrock of a new shared future.'

After one of the young people had handed him a large metal oak leaf embossed with these words, Martin placed his pledge on the tree, alongside the 409 pledges that had been written by young people. Two junior ministers, Democratic Unionist Alastair Ross and Sinn Féin's Megan Fearon, also made pledges and added their leaves to the tree.

Martin places his pledge on the tree.

Martin left the exhibition centre waving to the appreciative audience and wearing a broad smile on his face. Teachers and pupils were stopping him all the way to the exit to have selfies taken with him.

I was thrilled with how the day had gone. The huge gathering from across the nine counties and the showcasing of the young people's talents confirmed that young people are capable and ready for peace building. The feedback from civic, religious and political leaders, and from school principals, was universally positive, and strengthened my conviction that we were right in turning to our young people. The journey with them had to continue.

So happy to see Martin at the annual Bloody Sunday commemoration service at Rossville Street in January 2017.

14

A Man at Peace

The announcement by the Executive Office that, due to 'unforeseen personal circumstances', Martin would not be joining First Minister Arlene Foster on a planned ministerial visit to China (scheduled to begin on Monday 5 December 2016) was a bit of a surprise. It wasn't Martin's form to miss such an important trip but I didn't read too much into it.

A few days later, a group of thirty ministers and pastors from around Northern Ireland and from different parts of America paid a visit to First Derry to see the refurbished church and to hear first-hand about my friendship with Martin. After a cup of tea in the hall we moved to the church where the group sat listening to the – at times bumpy – journey Martin and I had been making together. At the end of the talk and after a stimulating Q&A session, I invited the group to pray for Martin, whom I knew wasn't well. What followed was both emotional and heart-warming. The prayers were filled with admiration and appreciation for the role Martin had played as peacemaker.

The next morning, to encourage Martin, I texted him: *Martin, a group of 30 clergy from NI & USA asked to meet with me yesterday @ 1st Derry. They wanted to hear about our friendship. At the end of my talk, 7 of the group prayed aloud for you, for me, for our city and for a new shared future. It was a heavenly moment. It's lovely to know people care enough to pray.*

God bless you Martin and keep you strong. Best to you, Bernie and family. David.

A short time later, I received the following reply from Martin: *Many thanks my friend, much appreciated, especially the prayers. Haven't been well recently and have undergone some tests to establish the problem. Nice to hear of the visitors to 1st Derry, so kind of them and you to pray for us there. Bernie and I send all our best wishes and love to you Margaret and family. God bless. M.*

My contact continued with Martin via text messaging. In the interim, the political situation in Northern Ireland had taken a turn for the worse after Sinn Féin and the DUP became embroiled in a bitter row over an energy incentive scheme championed by Arlene Foster. Sinn Féin called for the First Minister to step aside to allow for independent inquiries, but she refused. The dispute deepened when Arlene Foster made a statement before the Assembly on 19 December without Martin's approval (as required under the power-sharing agreement), resulting in Sinn Féin and the opposition parties all walking out of the Assembly. Things were not looking so good.

On Tuesday 20 December, I sent a text which read: *Martin, wanted to let you know in the course of my work today, I've been asked by many to let you know they are praying for you … So many are appreciating your leadership … Let all of this encourage you. The peace of the Lord be with you. David.*

It wasn't long until I received a reply: *Hi David, difficult times, grateful for all prayers. Politically important to make a bit of space to find a way forward out of this sorry mess. I'm in hospital at the moment but anxious to come up with a solution. Happy Christmas to you and Margaret. Warmest best wishes. God Bless my friend. M*

The next time I contacted Martin was on Monday 9 January – the day he announced his resignation as deputy

First Minister. *Martin, it can't have been easy for you stepping down as DFM earlier today. You have played such a pivotal role in bringing us to where we currently are. Moving into partnership with Ian at Stormont was a divinely guided decision. Many from our two traditions are truly grateful for your peace-building leadership. 'BLESSED ARE THE PEACEMAKERS FOR THEY SHALL BE CALLED SONS OF GOD.' Very best wishes, my true friend. David.*

The following day, I received a short text from Martin, which simply said: *David, many thanks my dear friend. Love to Margaret. M.*

© George Sweeney

Greeting my good friend.

Since 2010, a fixed date in my diary has been the annual service at the Bloody Sunday monument, to remember the loved ones who were so cruelly torn away from their families in January 1972. As I weaved through the crowd in the Bogside on my way to the service in 2017, I suddenly saw a tall figure in a long black overcoat. It was Martin. Approaching him from behind, I tapped him on the shoulder. Glancing around and seeing who it was, his face lit up. 'David, how are you, my friend?' he said, and we hugged. Martin looked healthy and sounded happy. I was pleased and relieved to see him this way.

Time marched on and I heard that the treatment Martin was receiving was working and everyone, including me, remained hopeful.

At the start of March, I was introduced to Baroness Paisley, and enjoyed a conversation with her, which focused especially on the remarkable friendship between Martin and her late husband. She spoke very highly of Martin, and I wanted to update Martin about this visit so I sent him a text message: *Martin, on Saturday morning I spent over two hours with Eileen Paisley. You were frequently brought into the conversation. What a difference both Ian and you made and what an example your friendship and partnership continues to be. It was lovely meeting you at the Bloody Sunday service. You continue to be in my prayers and in the thoughts of so many ... Maybe sometime soon we'll get a few minutes together. May God's blessing descend upon you, Bernie and your family and never leave you. David.*

The next day, I received the following text: *Bernie here. I have Martin's phone at the minute. He's in ICU. A lot of things are going on. God love him. Keep praying for him. Thank you for your kind words. Much appreciated.*

I had known Martin was in hospital but I was shocked that he was in intensive care – it was clear that the situation was graver than I had realised.

I had deliberately stayed away from the hospital until then, because I felt that Martin would want most to be with his family, but the day after I received Bernie's text I made my way to Altnagelvin Hospital and to the ICU. My idea was to connect with some of the McGuinness family to assure them of my thoughts and prayers for Martin. I asked a nurse who had just emerged from ICU if she would ask a member of Martin's family to meet me in the corridor.

A few moments later the door into a private room opened and a man approached me and said, 'I'm Martin's brother, Declan.' He warmly shook my hand. I told him that I'd come simply to offer my support to the family. Declan replied, 'Martin knows you are here and he wants to see you. You and him must have something special. I'm not sure Gerry Adams got in to see him!'

Entering the room, I could see Martin sitting up in the bed. A table had been drawn up in front of him and on it was his laptop. Seeing me, his face came alive with a broad happy smile. I went over to the bed and we firmly shook hands. In fact, for the duration of my visit we held each other's hand. I began by telling him, 'I was with Eileen Paisley last Saturday. She sends her best wishes and is praying for you. We talked a lot about Ian and you.'

Martin interjected, 'They're good people, David.'

I replied, 'And you're a good person, too. Ian and you did great things together. The two of you showed the rest of us what we should be doing.'

Our conversation continued with Martin sharing some information with me about his illness and the treatment he was receiving. He was full of admiration for the hospital staff. For the duration of my visit, Declan stood silently watching from a corner of the room. When we'd finished talking, I said to Martin, 'I'm going to pray.' As we held hands, I leaned in towards him to pray. There was an atmosphere and an energy in the room, which I have rarely ever experienced in all my years as a parish minister. At the end of my prayer he said, 'David, there's still more work to do.' When I came to leave it was hard to let go of his hand.

Before leaving, I stood for a moment or two at the foot of Martin's bed. His face was rapt with brightness. I was transfixed. A divine presence was in the room. He was peaceful and perfectly serene.

It was the last time I was to see my dear friend alive.

Declan accompanied me into the corridor. Noticing tears in my eyes, he said, 'David, Martin might look ill to you but all the stats are good; he's going to be okay.' Then he said something quite beautiful. 'David, that was a very precious moment you shared.' He was right; it was precious. Clearly Martin's body was weak but his spirit was strong.

For the next ten days, I kept in touch with Declan, who had kindly given me his mobile number. I had, for my own part, received many enquiries from both Catholics and Protestants, about Martin's health. Amongst these was a telephone call from former Ulster Unionist leader Lord Trimble. Ringing from London, he wanted to know how Martin was.

On Sunday 19 March I sent a text message to Declan: *Continuing to think of you all. Many people are remembering Martin from my community and tradition. Assure him of many prayers. Kind regards. David.*

Declan replied: *David the fight goes on – the medics are happy with his daily stats – hopefully they'll keep going in the right direction. Thanks for your kind thoughts.*

To everyone's surprise, Martin's condition changed dramatically and, in the early hours of Tuesday 21 March, he slipped away from Bernie and his family into the peace of eternity.

I sent a text message to Declan saying, *So, so sad. Hearts are heavy this morning across Ireland as the news of Martin's death breaks. You are all in my prayers. Speak later. David.*

The speed with which Martin's life ended was not what those closest to him expected. Up until a few hours before he closed his eyes for the last time, everyone had remained hopeful.

Martin's coffin is brought home.

As soon as I had finished my commitments at church, I rushed down to the Bogside, just in time to join a large crowd accompanying Martin's coffin back to his home. I was touched by the exceptional welcome I received – a great many hands reached out to shake mine. I was astonished by the sheer volume of people – it was on a scale that I had never before witnessed.

The next evening, I returned to Martin's home to meet with his family and offer them my condolences. Parking my car at a distance from the family home, I began walking up towards the house. The footpath was filled with people of all ages making their way to Martin's wake.

Rounding the corner into his street, I could not believe

the number of people converging on the family home. People were spilling off the footpath on to the road. Stewards wearing fluorescent vests were shepherding everyone into a long queue so as to file in by the front door in an orderly fashion, past Martin's coffin, and out into the street by a side door.

I was about to make my way to the end of the queue when someone said to me: 'Reverend, you don't need to join the queue, come with me.' I was taken straight into the sitting room where Martin's coffin was on display and his family were gathered. I have never seen a house so thronged with people; a river of mourners flowing through the McGuinness home to pay their respects. This was a massive outpouring of grief by a shocked community.

I recall being introduced to Martin's sister Geraldine who was standing beside her brother's coffin. 'Geraldine,' I said, 'I'm for giving you a hug because your brother often gave me a hug.'

After hugging, she pointed to a family photograph hanging on the wall that included her late mother, Peggy, and said: 'That's who he got it from; our mother was a hugger!'

While I was at the house Declan asked me if I would participate in Martin's Requiem Mass the following day in the Long Tower Catholic church. I was honoured but I realised that I would need to reflect very carefully on what I was going to say. Most of all, I wanted to provide peace, comfort and hope to the family.

At the same time, a number of journalists had been in touch with me, keen to interview me about Martin and our friendship. I accepted — while the media tended to focus on Martin's past, I wanted to draw attention to the person I knew he had become, while neither skirting around his role in the Troubles or minimising the hurt of victims and survivors.

Speaking at Martin's Requiem Mass at Long Tower Church.

15

Heaven Touches Earth

I had worked late into the night on my script for the church service. An hour before the service was due to begin, I travelled into the city and across the Craigavon Bridge. I had previously arranged to park my car in the parochial house car park on Abercorn Road. Reaching the end of the bridge and seeing the line of cars sitting bumper to bumper all the way to the top of Abercorn Road, I decided to abandon that plan and drive to First Derry's car park via Carlisle Road and the Diamond. Traffic moved slowly. Pedestrians, and there were lots of them, were moving faster on the footpath. I had never seen the city so busy – this was unprecedented.

People, who had parked their cars in every available space around the city, were hurriedly converging on the Diamond and onwards to Bishop Street to complete the journey to the church. Eventually reaching First Derry, I proceeded to collect my robes and begin the walk to the Long Tower church. The wide pavements in Bishop Street were filled with people. Everyone was moving in the same direction. Unlike any other funeral I have ever attended, this one had people in high-vis vests controlling and directing the huge crowds. There was a mixture of public pride and private grief as thousands of mourners from across the city and beyond joined with politicians and dignitaries from Ireland, Britain and the USA. There was only one destination and that was Martin's funeral service.

A great swell of people had gathered around the Long Tower church. Thankfully, close to the church railings, I was recognised by someone who ushered me into the comparative calm of the sacristy.

After robing and receiving instructions as to where I would sit during the service and when I would speak, conversation continued with my Roman Catholic clerical colleagues. As the only Protestant minister in the sacristy, I was welcomed with great warmth and dignity, and felt at home. There followed a lengthy wait – regular updates were relayed into the sacristy regarding the location of the funeral cortège, which was being held up due to the massive crowds of mourners. This gave me the opportunity to ask one of the priests to help me improve the pronunciation of the Irish words I planned to include in my eulogy.

Our conversation was abruptly interrupted by the sound of applause coming from inside the church. What started softly, quickly grew louder. We checked the monitors in the sacristy to ascertain the cause of the clapping but we couldn't work it out. Soon the mystery was solved as we were informed that Arlene Foster, the former First Minister and DUP leader, had taken her seat in the church. Her arrival had been greeted by resounding applause. A prominent Protestant politician in a Catholic church receiving the full generosity of nationalists and republicans in Derry. It was clear people wanted Arlene Foster to know they appreciated her being there.

When the coffin had been received into the church, I took up my place, along with officiating priests, in the sanctuary. Being invited into the sanctuary as a Protestant minister was a gracious gesture from my Catholic colleagues. From where I was sitting, I could easily identify high-profile political figures, past and present, assembled alongside ordinary men and women who had made the trip to Derry, from near and far, to honour their man. Inside the ornate building, every seat was occupied. It was beautiful to behold.

Parish Administrator Father Aidan Mullan, who I was sitting next to, periodically leaned across to helpfully whisper into my ear the relevance and significance of the liturgy being used. I appreciated this commentary and the way it made me feel included. Even during the celebration of the sacrament, which Protestants are prohibited from receiving, I didn't feel excluded – this aspect of Martin's Requiem Mass was administered in such a way that it was not divisive, which is a great credit to the organisers of the service.

During the service, Father Michael Canny invited me to address the congregation. At the time, I hadn't realised the international interest in the service. In any case, my main intention was to connect with Bernie, along with Martin's daughters, Fionnuala and Grainne, and sons, Emmett and Fiachra, and to provide them with comfort and hope.

According to the Old Testament book of Ecclesiastes (chapter 3, verse 11), 'God has set eternity in the hearts of men'. It's a longing that won't go away. It's why the ancient Egyptians built the pyramids and the ancient Greeks put a coin under the tongue of the departed so that they could pay the ferryman to cross the River Styx. Martin didn't want more of the same – he wanted what was wrong to be put right; he wanted suffering to stop; he wanted sectarianism and violence to become things of the past; he wanted a better future for everyone. In other words, Martin wanted heaven, which, as I said to Bernie and her family, is what he finally got.

Baroness Paisley put it beautifully when, in one of our conversations, she referred to life on the far side of the grave by saying, 'Heaven will be full of surprises. We'll be surprised by the absence of people we expected to see, and equally surprised by the people we never expected to see.' I concluded my eulogy by saying that at some point in the future, I looked forward, by God's grace, to being with Martin in the heavenly places.

That's a topic Bernie and I have returned to on a number of occasions since the funeral. Heaven is the Christian's eternal home and resting place, regardless of creed or culture. Knowing there will be reunions with those we have loved and lost is profoundly comforting and hopeful, particularly for those who remain and who mourn.

Many people since have spoken to me about Martin's funeral. Two thousand mourners packed inside the church, while an innumerable number stood outside listening to music, prayers, readings, tributes and Bill Clinton's speech, all marking the sadness and solemnity of the occasion. Lofty job titles, badges of office and labels of identity all drifted into the background and somehow it seemed like heaven touched earth, allowing a city and a country in mourning to glimpse what is possible when people, regardless of what they look like or how they pray, come together. It offered a moment in time that would be remembered; a moment expanding beyond politics and partisanship; a moment that set aside the reasons we use to look down on others and separate ourselves from one another; a moment confirming that, as the psalmist wrote, 'weeping may endure for a night but joy comes in the morning'.

Following the funeral, letters of appreciation for my

tribute to Martin during the Requiem Mass, including one from Sinn Féin President Gerry Adams, arrived, as well as text messages and emails. However, not everyone was as happy with my attendance and funeral tribute. Four families at First Derry stopped attending Sunday worship as a direct result of my participation in the service. In the weeks and months that have elapsed since that sad day, I have been approached by complete strangers, in places as far apart as Bangor, Enniskillen and Newry, who have thanked me for my part in Martin's funeral and also for my honest appraisal of him during television appearances around the time of his death.

During the church service I expressed my hope of seeing Martin McGuinness in the next world, and that has been a pill too hard to swallow for some, which I confess is understandable. The debate will long continue as to whether his violent past can be set aside in the light of his last peace-making decade. In my eyes, turning away from terrorism restored options for Martin, which he grasped readily, using his considerable influence for good. He lived out that last decade as a person who had experienced forgiveness. Refusing to remain married to the status quo, he decided to travel in a new direction and break new ground. In the words of Bill Clinton, 'he made honourable compromises and was strong enough to keep them and came to be trusted because his word was gold.'

With Martin, outside First Derry.

16

Sorely Missed, Fondly Remembered

In the time since Martin's death, I have felt his loss profoundly, and have reflected a great deal on his life and our friendship. I remember the times we shared and one visit in particular often comes to mind.

On New Year's Day, 2016, Martin arrived at my front door with a colourful bunch of flowers for my wife, Margaret. We'd arranged to meet up to discuss the countrywide gathering of young people at Maze Long Kesh scheduled for International Peace Day. At the end of this meeting I suggested to Martin that, as we were stepping out into the unknown of another year, it might be wise to start it with a prayer. We stood facing each other as I asked for God's blessing for Peter Robinson and Martin as First and deputy First Ministers, the Executive, the Assembly and the peace process. I continued by praying a blessing on Martin's wife Bernie and his family. Speaking into this prayer, I heard Martin's voice – he was asking God to bless me, my wife and my family. What a sublime moment for the two of us. When our joint prayer ended he said, 'David, I'm a Catholic Christian.'

I replied, 'Martin, I know exactly what you are saying. We're kindred spirits; we're both members of God's big worldwide family.'

Holocaust survivor Elie Wiesel wrote in *Souls on Fire*, 'When you die and go to meet your Maker, you're not going to be asked why you didn't become a Messiah or find a cure for cancer. All you're going to be asked is, "Why didn't you become you? Why didn't you become all that you are?"'

Fulfilling the role that has been mapped out for each one of us during our time on earth requires saying yes, first to our Maker and then to ourselves. Each one of us is unique – possessing talents, experiences and opportunities that no one else has ever had or ever will. By answering yes, Martin opened himself up to his God-given potential and to the greatest of possibilities. Some people will not concern themselves with such matters. They grind through their days without even lifting their eyes, choosing to live and die and never ask why.

Not so Martin McGuinness. Wanting his life to count, he altered his direction of travel to live in a way that made the world glad. When the possibilities for reconciliation appeared on the horizon, Martin McGuinness neither spurned them or turned them down. His approach to life can be summed up in the words of George Bernard Shaw: 'Other people see things and say, why? But I dream things that never were and ask, why not?'

After persuading the IRA to end its long war of attrition against the British, Martin went on to become a persistent persuader for peace, ending his career at the apex of a devolved government within the United Kingdom as a proud republican.

In the days and weeks that followed Martin's death, I was touched by the way people spoke to me about him. I first noticed this on the walls in Derry just hours after Martin's death. Along with lots of others, I was waiting to be interviewed by the many film crews that were assembling in the city. As I huddled in the darkness close to the Verbal Arts Centre, sheltering from the cold March wind, the tall figure of Sinn Féin President Gerry Adams approached me. Holding out his hand, he said, 'David, you have lost your friend.' His choice of words set a pattern for the way a great many thereafter extended their condolences to me.

These words from Gerry Adams marked the start of an avalanche – I have been amazed by the number of people who have approached me to speak about Martin and to express appreciation for his work towards inaugurating a new era for all.

In the course of these impromptu dialogues, people have said things like, 'It was great you both became friends', 'You got on so well together', 'Your friendship contributed to him becoming a different person', 'You must miss him' and, most frequently, 'Sorry you've lost your friend'. Other people have gone out of their way to comment on 'the gap that has been created by his death', 'the conspicuous absence of leadership in the country now that he's gone' and 'the political inertia his passing has generated'. Innumerable people, including seasoned unionist politicians, have remarked to me, 'If your friend had still been with us, Stormont would be up and running.'

Interestingly, many Catholics and Protestants have spoken about the relationship Martin McGuinness enjoyed with Ian Paisley and about their longing for another strong duo, with similar compatible chemistry, to emerge and emulate Martin's and Ian's enviable model of shared leadership.

A couple of months after Martin's death, I was stopped

one afternoon in Belfast by a tall, youthful man who, without any introduction, enquired: 'Are you the guy that's friendly with Martin McGuinness?' Not dressed as a clergyman and a bit wary about being recognised seventy-five miles from home left me unsure how to reply. But I decided to plough ahead.

'Yes, I'm David Latimer from Londonderry.'

The man continued, 'I'm a Protestant from Carrickfergus. I've got two children and I want them both to grow up in a peaceful Northern Ireland. I liked you for reaching out to Martin McGuinness; he was the one man who was able to understand both sides.'

I replied, 'That's a lovely thing you've just said about Martin. I will share what you've said with his wife Bernie.'

I was thrilled by what he'd said and so too was Bernie when I shared this story with her during a visit to her home.

Not everybody I bump into speaks so glowingly of Martin, and the charge that I am fawning over a former IRA commander has been levelled against me. Others were quick to proclaim that I was naive and being used by Sinn Féin. Those who frowned on my friendship with Martin seem to think I have conveniently forgotten about Martin's role in the IRA campaign of terror and that I am devoid of feelings for the bereaved and injured. Nothing could be further from the truth. I do not expect families who have suffered at the hands of the IRA to let go of their grief, which is human, natural and understandable. Nor do I wish, in any way, to cause further hurt to victims and survivors of IRA violence by appearing to airbrush Martin's past from the narrative.

The truth is that the harsh facts relating to anyone's

life can never ever be erased from the canvas. I understand entirely why many people have mixed feelings about Martin and my friendship with him. At the same time, though, I cannot disregard his achievements or those of Ian Paisley, for example, who changed immeasurably and compromised sufficiently to let a new future begin.

In the current global context of uncertainty, the transformation that has occurred in Northern Ireland since the signing of the Good Friday Agreement in 1998 is evidence that differences can be set aside in the interests of the common good and that, where the will exists, true change is possible.

To me, Martin McGuinness was more than the person who personally intervened to end the disruptive paint bomb attacks at First Derry. He was more than the person who influenced the Northern Ireland government to commit funding for the refurbishment of the Presbyterian Church in the Bogside. He was more than the person who championed the youth-led peace-building initiatives I was pioneering. He was more than a public representative for the Foyle Assembly constituency. He was more than the deputy First Minister of Northern Ireland. In fact, Martin was more to me than all of these – he was my friend.

On my mobile phone I have retained Martin's number. Even though no calls, no voicemails and no text messages have been received from this number since March 2017, my deliberate refusal to delete the number is one way I've chosen to keep his memory alive. Another, and much superior, way of holding on to the memory of times spent together is the continuing contact I have with Martin's wife Bernie and their children, Fionnuala, Grainne, Emmett and

Fiachra, and my regular visits to the McGuinness family home.

Sometimes on life's journey what is needed is a leap of faith. It is this that can turn out to be the longest, hardest and scariest move we'll ever have to take. All that is needed is one decision – such as the one I made more than a decade ago when I appealed on BBC Radio Foyle to the only person I believed could stop the paint-bomb attacks at my church.

Our most enduring regrets are those of inaction – the things that we could have done but chose not to. Choosing to trust God means that, after more than ten years, I can attest to harbouring no regrets in any shape or form.

At the close of a recent church service, one of First Derry's long-standing elders made a point of speaking with me: 'David, you have my total support for the work you are doing in our city to build better relations; I really mean this and urge you to continue; it's needed now more than ever.' That endorsement, from a man whose family roots are firmly fixed in the Maiden City, broadly reflects the mood in the church where I have had the honour of ministering for thirty years.

Despite reducing numbers attending Sunday worship, due in large part to my close links with Martin McGuinness, the steadfastness of 'the many' at First Derry who did not jump ship has emboldened me to persevere, and invigorated Martin, helping him to shape a different destiny for all.

Differences are important and cannot ever be ignored but our common humanity matters much more. The job in hand, therefore, for all of us, is to strengthen the commonality we share by weaving the threads of our differing beliefs and practices into the single fabric of a better and brighter future.

The template for this task is, thankfully, in place. Martin McGuinness has bequeathed it to us. In a recent reference to Martin, Tony Blair's former Director of Communications Alastair Campbell said: 'Some will never forget his past but without him there would be no peace.'

Bill Clinton expressed our role best when he said at Martin's Requiem Mass that we should 'honour his legacy by our living and finish the work that there is to be done.'

Across future generations, Martin McGuinness will, I believe, cast a shadow like no other political leader. The story of how we will remember him is only beginning to be written. In his own unique way, he embodied what we hoped our society might become. He navigated the politics of conflict and reconciliation with audacity and care. His learning curve should inspire today's leaders.

He gave me strength in time of trouble and wisdom in time of uncertainty. One hopes his spirit will endure. We have lost a special human being, such that I have never seen in my own lifetime. I miss him greatly.

He will always be by my side. And, for that, I will be eternally grateful.

> *Go raibh maith agat, Martin.*
> *Beannacht leat go bhfeicfidh mé arís thú.*
> *Ar dheis Dé go raibh a h'anam.*

APPENDIX 1

THE HOMECOMING THANKSGIVING SERMON

There was a clergyman who proved to be a bit wearisome due to his custom of always finding something to give thanks for. After a week of torrential rain his flock wondered what he could possibly give thanks for on Sunday. To their surprise he started the service with a prayer thanking God every week was not wet like this week!

It's good to give thanks, which is the reason that brings us to St Anne's Cathedral this afternoon. During our pre-deployment training we met in St Wilfrid Garrison church in York and there we committed ourselves to the Almighty for our journey into the unknown of an Operational Tour of Duty with HM Forces. Having returned home safely it is therefore right and proper for us to be in church and collectively express our thanks to the Maker and Protector of us all.

Now how can I, as your padre, go about formulating a big thank you to God? Well I'm for doing it by drawing your attention to something the metal-smith in Camp Bastion made for me; it's a cross – not the kind you would find in a religious shop. This one is made from six empty fifty-calibre cases. The impact of bullets, shells, IEDs and whatever else was used in the Afghan desert are all potentially deadly. In contrast to some movies that specialise in glamorising violence, the use of force – as we found out – results in physical disfigurement, the loss of limbs, severe pain and sometimes death.

It is true to say we've seen more than our share of horrific sights during our time in the desert. Injuries sustained by service-personnel as well as innocent Afghans, including children, will live long in our memories.

This cross of empty bullet cases vividly symbolises such things as the cruelty and death of life outside the perimeter walls of Camp Bastion. In contrast, inside those perimeter walls there was a world-class trauma hospital specialising in saving lives. All of you, along with those attached to the Hospital Squadron, had the enormous privilege of taking your skills and drills and, in the most unlikely of locations, treating a multitude of seriously wounded people and even bringing some back from the very edge of the grave. You showed to yourselves and the world another and altogether different side to the cross and that's the hope and the life it symbolises.

Reflecting on our time in Afghanistan's Helmand Province we intimately know how this cross can both represent the ugly pain and broken bodies of a theatre of war. But we also intimately know how this same cross depicts the mending of broken bodies and the hope of recovery for the injured. So, I hold before you a cross crafted from empty bullet cases which I believe assists us, even in some small way, to express our appreciation to God for the protection and security He surrounded us with and for the life-saving endeavours all of you were associated with, regardless of your cap badge or rank.

In conclusion, may I implore you not to limit your view of the cross to our human endeavours, however commendable and worthy they turn out to be. Rather lift up your eyes to catch sight of somebody bigger and better than all of us and the impressive work accomplished during Op Herrick 8. I'm referring, of course, to a man called Jesus whose connection with a cross long ago introduced the prospect of healing and hope for people of every creed and culture and not just for as long as they live but everlastingly.

Prayer:

O Christ the Master Carpenter, who at the last through wood and nails purchased man's whole redemption. Grant that as we come rough hewn to Thy bench we may there be fashioned to a truer beauty. Amen.

Note: this is the text of the sermon that I was not allowed to preach at the thanksgiving service at St Anne's Cathedral (see pages 29–31).

APPENDIX 2

ADDRESS FOR THE SINN FÉIN ARD FHEIS, 2011

A Cháirde. This, as you will know, is Irish for 'friends'. Intentionally I begin with this greeting because that is what I firmly believe we are becoming.

Martin, you and I have been journeying together for the past five years and during that time we have become very firm friends, able to relax in each other's company. While our interaction might, understandably, raise an eyebrow amongst some within our communities the reality is, you and I regard ourselves to be brothers within the same human family; a diverse worldwide family, which despite all its flaws and imperfections is loved by God, the Maker of everything that lives and moves.

Your invitation to me as a Protestant minister is forward-looking and timely. Is it possible Democratic Unionists, this year or next, could see their way to invite a Catholic priest to address their Party conference? I'd like to think my co-religionists would emulate what you have done, not for cheap publicity; rather in recognition, despite our respective Dublin/London preferences, that our destinies are tied up together and our futures are bound together. Ladies and gentlemen, this means we can no longer continue to walk alone: the more we do together, both as ordinary people on the street and as politicians on 'the Hill', the better we will shape our shared future.

The seeds of division and enmity that have long characterised Catholic and Protestant relations were neither sown in 1968 or 1921 but during the 1609 Settlement of Ulster. Mistrust and bad feelings resulting in the Colonisation of Ireland by Protestant settlers were followed by centuries of political and social segregation. Partitioning Ireland did little to ease sectarian mistrust and separateness between Catholics and Protestants left in 'the six counties,' as each community continued to be defined by its particular religious affiliation with little mixture between the two groups. Little wonder this part of Ireland descended into a spiral of communal disorder and violence that was to last for three decades! Victims of differences extending back across endless centuries that have isolated us from one another, it is, with the benefit of historical hindsight, not surprising that our two communities should view each other with suspicion and regard one another as 'the enemy'.

Locked into our separate 'comfort zones' of isolation and poor relations we miserably failed to understand one other or do anything about each other's grievances. A 1993 report to the General Assembly of the Presbyterian Church in Ireland makes for interesting reading. 'The Presbyterian Church in Ireland shares the guilt of the majority community in Northern Ireland for tolerating the practice of discrimination in jobs, housing and voting rights, which largely led to the Civil Rights Campaign in the late 1960s.' Was the penny, albeit fifteen years into the Troubles, finally starting to drop? Was my community admitting that sins of omission could be as damaging as sins of commission? I rather like a comment by Marcus Aurelius, the last of the five good emperors, who during the second century wrote, 'A wrongdoer is often one who has left something undone – not always one who has done something'

Ladies and gentlemen, it is my considered opinion that by our silence and by our actions we have together contributed to perpetuating the divisions created long ago that progressively plunged us deeper into chaos and turmoil. This analysis I'm sharing with you means there is no one, whether Orange or Green, who can lift an accusing finger to apportion blame and that's because all of us, to a greater or lesser extent, have been part of the problem in some shape or form!

But let's move the story forward. A drained population, longingly waiting for a streak of light that one day might break through the clouds and offer a glimmer of hope to soothe their sorrows and heal their wounds, couldn't believe the news that broke on Tuesday 8th May 2007. This was the story of the most unlikely political marriage between Democratic Unionists and Sinn Féin. Photographs of Ian Paisley and Martin McGuinness standing side by side as the newly elected First and deputy First Ministers of the power-sharing Stormont Assembly were breathtaking.

In these epic scenes, that none of us will easily forget, Martin, you and Ian lit a candle of hope enabling Catholics and Protestants, nationalists and unionists, loyalists and republicans to envision the snow melting and winter turning to summer. No longer would our two communities need to drink from the cup of bitterness; no longer would it be necessary for them to blame and endlessly complain about each other; no longer would anyone, British or Irish, need to wallow in the valley of despair. Certainly not. Two very different communities could, at long last, anticipate standing as equals on the warm threshold of a better and brighter new day.

Moving the story even further forward we can identify what can best be described as groundbreaking strides bravely taken by the top layer of our government. Well, how else can we explain the First Minister's decision to visit a Catholic church and the attendance by the deputy First

Minister at the same church on the same day for the funeral mass of a murdered PSNI officer? On that very sad day GAA Officials agreeably passed Constable Ronan Kerr's coffin to PSNI Officers. Clearly history was being made and the narrative was being recorded, not on separate sheets of paper but on the same page and that was something that had not previously happened. Furthermore, we cannot overlook President McAleese and Queen Elizabeth standing side by side in Dublin's Garden of Remembrance to honour those who died fighting for Irish independence and remaining together for not just one National Anthem but for both! Makes you think, does it not, that two heads of state espousing different allegiances were showing all of us it is time to shake free the restricting chains of history.

During this weekend you will discuss and explore a raft of issues that relate to people of all ages such as education, health, housing, inward investment, justice and equality. While progress in each of these arenas will be beneficial, it must be emphasised the no political party in the North can dismiss searching for that hitherto elusive ingredient, which is nothing more or nothing less than salve for the hurting people who live in every council area and in each Assembly constituency.

This means, I believe, that despite all our progress and our prospects for the future everything that will be achieved will never be fully appreciated by everyone because of our tendency to postpone turning to our dark and terrible past. As a clergyman I only wish I could somehow provide victims, in both our communities, with a ready-mix-and-stir formula that would relieve their pain and wipe away their tears. Regretfully, that is beyond the ability of any mortal individual to deliver. However, it would be helpful for broken and bruised people to know it is acceptable for bereaved Protestants to articulate a story of the past and for bereaved Catholics also to articulate a story of the past. While both sets of stories will not be the same, each story needs to be recognised as real and personal. Therefore rather than airbrush personal stories of hurt there is a collective requirement for a spirit of maturity to be fostered whereby it will be possible for different stories pertaining to the past to be fairly acknowledged.

This could offer more than a modicum of comfort to our hurting families living in both Catholic and Protestant neighbourhoods, although I very much doubt it will be sufficient, which prompts me to suggest that OFMDFM explore devising a framework that would lead to A COUNTRY-WIDE DAY FOR HOPE & TRANSFORMATION. Such a solitary public event would provide a space and a time for everyone involved in the conflict to acknowledge the pain each has inflicted. Admitting we have hurt each other and that we have been hurt by each other and need to forgive one another would undeniably be liberating for the island of Ireland.

Our religious and political differences will prevail but compared to the benefits of peace they will be relatively trivial. Therefore, for the sake of our children, we must keep moving forward together. We must not let the peace die. With Almighty God's help we all can have a distinguished future where we will work and grow in harmony, and not just for a particular political cause, but for the greater good of all.

I would now like to offer a prayer for you all:

> May the Lord show His mercy up on us
> May the light of His presence be our guide
> May He guard and uphold us;

May His spirit be ever at our side
When we sleep may His angels watch over us
When we wake may He fill us with His grace
May we love Him and serve Him all our days
Then in heaven may we see His face,
Through Jesus Christ our Lord. Amen.

Ádh mór ort ... and God bless you all ... and God bless Ireland, North, South, East and West.

APPENDIX 3

FUNERAL EULOGY

I am grateful for this opportunity to speak a few words about my very good friend Martin McGuinness. We first met on the front steps of First Derry Presbyterian Church in the autumn of 2007. Across the years Martin and I got to know each other, to like each other and to trust each other.

Bernie, this is a very difficult time for you and your family. I'm for sharing a lovely true story with you, Grainne, Fionnuala, Fiachra and Emmett, which epitomises the kind of man your husband was. This story is situated in the middle of the 2013 UK City of Culture celebrations. Martin Luther King III, son of the great dreamer Dr Martin Luther King Jnr, was due to visit our city. I travelled down to Belfast International Airport in a stretch limousine, kindly provided by local undertakers Adair & Neely. After picking up Mr King and his two colleagues we made our way to Stormont Castle to meet with both the First and deputy First Ministers. The meeting, with Martin and Peter in the First Minister's Office couldn't have been better. On the way back to Derry one of Mr King's travelling companions, a lady called Beni who had been a life-long confidant to Mrs Coretta Scott King, announced excitedly from the rear seat of the limousine, 'David I'm getting a great feeling about Martin McGuinness. That man has a good heart!' And that of course was true. But not only did Martin have a good heart; he had a big heart and that enabled him to reach out to friends and foes alike.

Martin has bequeathed to us a better place to live. It was

his passion to create a new order of cooperation where we would live in relationship, not out of relationship and get to know one another.

We must together pledge to keep on doing what he was doing and to persevere in the pursuit of peace.

Today we thank God for Martin McGuinness. At some point in the future we shall, by God's amazing grace, praise God with him in the heavenly places.

Go raibh míle maith agat, Martin.

ACKNOWLEDGEMENTS

I am indebted to a small but special group of people, without whom this book would not have been possible.

I cannot thank my friends at the *Derry Journal* enough for their willingness to travel with me. My first visit to the *Journal*'s office was to plant the seed of a book devoted to my friendship with Martin McGuinness. The idea secured editor Arthur Duffy's immediate support. Arthur pledged to provide whatever resources and support I would need, including the services of one of his journalists, Sean McLaughlin.

I knew Sean and had long admired his skilful writing. Articles appearing in the *Derry Journal* under his name were consistently well crafted and compulsive reading. From the outset I was reassured that I was in the company of the best and all would be well.

Sean organised and retrieved a mass of material relating to Martin and me from *Journal* archives. He wisely recommended a timeline for this material and continuously offered valuable advice. Much of my original writing was reshaped by Sean, insomuch as he seemed to know me and what I wanted to say better than I did. Sean also selected photographs that captured moments described in the book.

My two congregations of God's people at First Derry Presbyterian Church and Monreagh Presbyterian Church in County Donegal are deserving of my utmost praise for persevering and tolerating me, particularly when I reached out to Martin McGuinness. Very few Presbyterian Meeting Houses would have been so supportive of their minister. Unswerving encouragement from my elders in both churches was tantamount to a breeze for my sail and fuel for my tank and, for that, I will always be grateful.

I am enormously grateful to President Bill Clinton for providing an endorsement for the book, and to Gerry Adams TD who helped to facilitate this. President Clinton's comments are testament to the friendly relations he and Martin enjoyed over many years.

Writing a book in addition to pastoring two congregations progressively eats into family and relationship time. To my family and especially my long-suffering wife Margaret, who is endowed with considerable patience, I offer my heartfelt thanks.

The willingness of Blackstaff Press and particularly Patsy Horton, Managing Editor, to print and publish this book cannot be underestimated. Neither can the close support provided by Senior Editor Helen Wright and all she did to keep the book moving. Her professional advice, empathy, enviable skill with expressive language and adeptness in word arrangement have all meant so much.

Finally, I wish to express delight in the continuing friendship I enjoy with the McGuinness family. I am ever so pleased that this book, which focuses on Martin, was commissioned with his wife Bernie's personal blessing. Her foreword to the book is, in itself, a treasure and adds to the authenticity of a deep friendship between two men who were willing to take a leap of faith.